WANASEMA:

Conversations with African Writers

T0307872

WANASEMA:

Conversations with African Writers

Editor: Don Burness

Associate Editor: Mary-Lou Burness

Ohio University Center for International Studies
Africa Studies Program

Monographs in International Studies
Africa Series Number 46

Athens, Ohio 1985

Library of Congress Cataloging in Publication Data
Main entry under title:

Wanasema: Conversations with African writers.

(Monographs in international studies. Africa series ; no. 46)
Bibliography: p.
1. Authors, African—Interviews. 2. African literature—History
and criticism—Addresses, essays, lectures. I. Burness, Donald.
II. Burness, Mary-Lou. III. Series.
PL8010.C65 1985   809' .889'6   85-5064
ISBN 0-89680-129-2
Reprinted 1987.

ISBN: 0-89680-129-2

For my African friends who went out of
their way to make me feel at home –

        Chinua and Christie Achebe

        Chidi and Ngozi Maduka

            and

        Obi Maduakor

TABLE OF CONTENTS

PREFACE

When I decided to do a series of interviews with African
writers I had a distinct set of priorities. I wanted the interviews to be spontaneous and if possible exciting. I wanted them
to be personal portraits of the writers as well. I did not want
to ask a series of detailed questions about individual characters
in individual books, because I find such exercises both dull and
sterile. I wanted these conversations to be of interest both to
the serious student of African literature and to the general
reader. For this reason I approached the interviews without
writing down questions in advance although I did have general
areas I wanted to explore. As a result the conversations tend to
have a life of their own.

To encourage open conversation I chose in most instances
not to use a tape recorder, for I felt that the intrusion of the
machine can inhibit natural dialogue. In fact, one writer insis-
ted that he would only do an interview if no tape recorder was
present. I was very fortunate to have the assistance of my wife,
Mary-Lou, who is an accomplished stenographer. She was present
at all the interviews conducted in English and captured as
closely as is humanly possible the exact rendering of each conversation. Of course 100% accuracy is impossible so typed copies
of these interviews were sent to each writer, who was free to
make any corrections he or she wished.

A tape recorder was used for interviews conducted in French
with Aminata Sow Fall of Senegal and in Portuguese with Manuel
Lopes of Cape Verde. I myself translated these conversations
into English. In my first interview in French with Nkulngui
Mefana of Cameroon there was no recorder so I wrote down each
sentence as I heard it. This made for a painfully slow and most
unnatural dialogue. I decided that I would have to use a recorder in further foreign language interviews.

Because a series of interviews can present only a synecdo-
chic image of the African literary world, I set out to explore
as many different landscapes as I could. For that reason I
chose to interview writers who express themselves in French,
Portuguese and English. I also made a specific point to interview at least one author, Samson Amali, of Nigeria, who, rooted
in oral tradition, writes in an indigenous African language. I
met with novelists, dramatists, poets. I met with writers both
Christian and Moslem. I met with two of the leading women writers, one from West Africa, the other from East Africa. I met
with writers old and young. The fact that a majority of the
interviews are with Nigerian authors stems from the fact that I
spent much more time in Nigeria than in any other country in Africa. But even there I attempted to speak with important writers, famous and not so famous, who came from different societies and who are planting different crops. In other words, I
I have tried, through individual conversations, to present not
only a portrait of individual authors, but an inquiry into dif-

1

ferent dimensions and concerns of modern African writing. Taken
together, the interviews attest to the diversity of African literature.

One final point. Fortune plays a large part in a book such
as this. Some writers I hoped to interview were unavailable.
One country, Cape Verde, denied me a visa. One writer I particularly wanted to interview broke appointments on two occasions
after I had flown hundreds of miles to meet with him. Neverthe-
less, I feel that I was very fortunate to be able to meet so many
writers, who were kind enough to spend time with me, and I only
hope that they enjoyed my company as much as I enjoyed theirs.

Don Burness

ELECHI AMADI

Elechi Amadi, a retired civil servant, is most noted for his three novels, THE CONCUBINE, THE GREAT PONDS and THE SLAVE, as well as his personal essay on the Civil War, SUNSET IN BIAFRA. All are published in the African Writers Series by Heinemann. He has also written four plays and most recently published ETHICS IN NIGERIAN CULTURE. I have admired him because he tells a good story and does so without wasting words.

I first met Elechi by chance in his village of Aluu while I was attending a wrestling match in mid November, 1982. I was in the process of writing an essay on the theme of wrestling in African literature and wanted very much to see an actual wrestling festival. Moreover, as a basketball and tennis coach I like sporting events of all kinds. I met Elechi on four or five other occasions while I was in Nigeria. We were not strangers in each other's homes.

At first Elechi was reluctant to grant an interview. I had been told that he does not grant interviews. But his sense of African hospitality eventually became stronger than his reticence. On the day of the interview, Elechi took me to see several shrines in Aluu and also gave me palm wine to drink at his home. The actual interview took place in the late afternoon of February 17, 1983 in my residence at the University of Port Harcourt in Choba, Rivers State, Nigeria.

ELECHI AMADI

Q. I have a feeling that the village world you write about is not just a world of a different age, that Aluu still exists today as a village community.

A. Yes, it certainly exists. We still have the same values, ceremonies and festivities, so part of that world definitely exists.

Q. Your novels are portraits of Aluu. The great ponds, the shrine of Amadioha, the wrestling arena, the characters – these can be found today.

A. Yes, but the names are all different in my novels.

Q. John Munonye said in our interview that the village is dead. There is no more village. He said "I went back home and it was gone."

A. I don't think it's strictly true for Aluu. I have the feeling of the village when I go there and very strongly. Like last weekend when I was at a burial ceremony. Of course you have the inroads of modern civilization – lots of people working in town, television. You can see the inroads. But the village spirit is intact for now. But I don't think it will be so for long.

Q. This is not true in all parts of Nigeria.

A. I can't speak for all parts of Nigeria, but among the Ikwerre, village life is still very much alive.

Q. Wrestling is still alive in Aluu?

A. Very much so, as you know.

Q. And it is a total communal experience. And you like wrestling and write about it. Did you consciously set out in writing books about wrestling to depict the wrestler – his relationship to the community, the psychology of the athlete, etc.?

A. Not really. The point is I was fortunate in being brought up in the village. For the first twelve years of my life I was in the village and imbibed a lot of the spirit of the village. So when I decided to write about the village – things like wrestling, the power of the gods, they just came naturally. Without these things the village scene would disappear. I don't make a conscious effort to project these things. They are an integral part of the village life as I know it.

4

Q. There are two kinds of wrestling in your work – wrestling in the arena and wrestling with the gods.

A. Wrestling is used to depict struggle.

Q. You were trained as a scientist in physics and math. I am wondering if that has had an effect on your writing. In your novels, in your recent book ETHICS IN NIGERIAN CULTURE, you strive for objectivity – a disinterested view of the world. Is that a correct perception?

A. Yes. I think I strive for realism in my novels. I try not to intrude as much as I can. Of course, editorial intrusion is unavoidable, but people tell me there's a certain terseness and precision in the way I write. This is what they say. I don't know. They tend to attribute this to my scientific training. I just write as I can.

Q. Chinua Achebe was initially admitted to Ibadan as a student of chemistry while John Munonye, who also has a tight style, is a classicist, so I don't think we can therefore equate terseness of style with specific academic training. There are many African writers who choose to intrude. In fact, they tend to intrude so much that you are more aware of the writer than you are of his characters. These writers are frequently called committed. They are politically involved. Such a writer will remind the reader what he is supposed to be thinking as he reads. Do you think this makes for good art?

A. I think it doesn't and I made this quite clear in a paper "The Problem of Commitment in Literature." I think that thoroughgoing commitment doesn't make for literature of the highest quality. Now and then some real geniuses are able to transcend and write masterpieces but for the mediocre writer commitment is a big problem. The more he gets into commitment the more he has to work out so many different problems apart from writing. I think really good writing should not be a committed expose of bad government, corruption, etc. You have armies of journalists all over the world writing about these things and they are doing it very well. I think the novel is a very inefficient way to talk about politics. The novelist should use his art for something better than talking about errors of government. It's like sweeping the streets with brooms of gold.

Q. Isn't "commitment" a loaded word? In other words, any writer has got to be committed to something, at least to language. Hasn't the word itself become abused and limited in the modern sense?

A. I had this thrown at me. I am regarded as a purist here in

Nigeria. People say "You are committed to traditional values, rural life. You are very committed." They say "everyone is committed." I say - O.K. broadly speaking, every writer is committed - universal values, truth, beauty, goodness, being your brother's keeper - all that. Every moral writer would consciously or unconsciously uphold these values. This is not what I mean by commitment. I'm talking specifically about a writer who goes all out to project a point of view or try to alter a political situation by propagating an ideology to which he is emotionally committed. His objective, therefore, looms very large and because of that he faces a lot of problems. You can't trust him because of his bias. So when he says - this is beautiful or powerful - you're not sure he means that. He loses objectivity. Then there is this other problem of overkill. Take Ayi Kwei Armah. I quarrel with his use of filth, of excrement, in THE BEAUTYFUL ONES ARE NOT YET BORN. There's terrible attention to detail. It's pornography. I find it very bad writing. He was so preoccupied with corruption in Ghana that he had to stoop down to that level. Orwell's 1984 is a very beautiful novel. The love affair is very poignant. But it is also a political novel. In one section, for about eleven pages, he goes on about the Marxist class struggle. He talks about upper class, middle class, lower class for eleven pages. I found that very tedious. If he wasn't so committed he wouldn't have gone to that level. That's one disadvantage of commitment - having people feel put upon. Reading the book I see the author trying to convince me. I feel put upon; I resent it. It's like an advertisement. I made this point. If the Mona Lisa had originally been an ad it would have been looked at as an ad. There's something in the human psyche. People feel it's not really inspiration as such and that devalues the painting because it has the purpose of selling a product. The same effect is produced in literature. I made these points in that article.

Q. Where was that article published?

A. I delivered it at the University of Calabar and later at the University of Port Harcourt. It was published in the students' paper at Calabar. I am sending it to KUNAPIPI in Aarhus.

Q. Your three novels, THE CONCUBINE, THE GREAT PONDS, and THE SLAVES have come out in the Heinemann African Writers Series. I came to Nigeria thinking you were just a novelist. Within a week of arriving, I turned on the T.V. and saw a production of THE ROAD TO IBADAN and underneath it said "A play by Elechi Amadi." I said to myself "I didn't know he wrote plays." And since then I discovered you've written three or four plays. These are plays that have appeared quite regularly on television in this country. You mentioned today that ISIBURU

6

was presented in front of General Gowon for FESTAC 1977. Do you want to talk a little about your plays?

A. Yes. I think I write plays for fun. When I go to the theatre I want to feel relaxed and enjoy myself. I hate plays that are terribly intense and very serious, with no humor, that tell you how bad the world is - we're going to hell - how terrible the human situation is. This may well be so, but I don't like these plays. I go to relax and enjoy myself. I'm not adverse to learning a thing or two about the state of the world, but I don't want to spend a whole evening being told we're going to hell. So when I write plays I have this at the back of my mind. I want people to laugh, feel life is good, enjoy themselves. A play like PEPPERSOUP is a lot of laughs. It satirizes a black and white marriage. From beginning to end it is laughs. ISIBURU was an epic poem but when I read it through I realized it had dramatic effect so all I did was introduce characters. THE ROAD TO IBADAN was born out of the war, of course. It has to do with two students cut off at the front. Again there is humor, but there had to be a bit of horrors of war. But it's a comedy as well. The girl marries an army officer en route. The most recent play is DANCER OF JOHANNESBURG. It's only been staged once or twice here. It focuses on the apartheid problem. I tried not to be committed in that play but I don't think I entirely succeeded! I tried as much as I could to be as uncommitted as possible and just give my viewers a good story. I think that because my plays are rather light hearted, because they are not teaching anybody anything, people think they are not very serious plays so I am regarded more as a novelist than as a playwright.

Q. Do you accept this point of view?

A. I really am quite indifferent. People enjoy them. When I meet a guy on the street and he says "I enjoyed PEPPERSOUP," that is my reward.

Q. You're also an essayist; SUNSET IN BIAFRA is a long, personal essay. It isn't easy to write humorously about that war. Has anything been gained from that war?

A. By whom?

Q. By Nigeria - by your village - by Africa?

A. Well, I think this is more a political question than literary. I think people learned some lessons, learned that selfishness does not pay. Better to be a large country. It's no good killing your brother. All courage and suffering normally come to naught as all wars teach us, and we never learn. All wars have been trying to teach us that all

7

conflicts are ultimately futile.

Q. Dostoevsky is torn between the theoretical need to love
humanity - what you just said - that we're all brothers,
that we must love one another or die - and the fact that he
doesn't like most individual human beings very much. You
don't seem to have been beaten down by disillusionment and
coming to terms with the world as it is. You seem to see
life as a song and as a good thing. I don't think that's all
that common in the modern world.

A. Many people think I have a tragic view of the world. I don't
know now whether to think I have the opposite.

Q. There can be affirmation in the tragic view. There are tragic views where there is merely a portrait of despair. You
have sympathy for your own characters. They are likeable
people. That to me is an assertion of humanity, an assertion
of life. That's what I meant. It doesn't preclude a tragic
view.

A. I think life is something to be cherished, even though we
don't understand it at all. But by and large, I think it's
something to be cherished and that while we're here we
should do our best to make the world a pleasant place.
That's about the best we can do. We don't know our fate ultimately, but while this picnic lasts, we should make the
best of it. But in the ultimate view, you cannot but have a
tragic view. The earth is very delicately balanced. It appears the earth is a comparatively isolated spaceship. If
anything happens to the earth, that's probably the end of
life in this galaxy. This could happen any moment. The at-
mosphere may evaporate. There are any number of calamities
that could happen. In that overview I don't see how anyone
could help having a tragic view. But while we are here it's
beautiful and we should make the best of it. During the war,
even when I was in prison and being tortured - I wasn't
really tortured but starved - it was still possible for me
to look at the world dispassionately. I could see the
guards starving me, see their little interests - the comic
element of human beings around me. After the war I was able
to write with what I hope was reasonable objectivity.

Q. In the West we are very much aware of Nigerian writers who
write in English. We are not aware of many writers writing
in Hausa, Ijaw, Igbo. Are these writers getting a fair
shake here in Nigeria? Is there proper encouragement?

A. I don't think they're getting enough publicity or enough
chances of getting their works published in the first place.
Publishing in this country is still in its infancy and even
existing companies don't have the capacity to print large
numbers. A Hausa writer of short stories has five thousand

8

copies of his work published and when it's finished, it's finished.

Q. Wouldn't it be the responsibility of Nigerian academics to support work by these writers and introduce them in their classes?

A. Very much so. The trouble is because of our colonial past we are very much English literature oriented; we are brought up on Shakespeare, Dickens, Hardy. In a paper I once delivered at Ibadan I made the point that here in Nigeria when people to go school they start them off with these writers and then they go to university and read more of these writers and it's only as a curiosity, at the tail end, that they read African authors, even in their post-graduate work. It should be the other way around. Our students should start with Nigerian literature in all the various languages, English included, of course. We are so much involved with the foreign we have no time to seek out pleasures in our own literature.

Q. This is changing, isn't it?

A. Very slowly.

Q. Do you think critics serve any useful purpose?

A. I have a lot of reservations. I do think they serve a useful purpose in that they bring out certain aspects of works of art to the level of appreciation, but I also think that they can be a sort of spoil-sport sometimes. You can read a really good book and then see critics put it down very badly. That's because they have worked out certain schemes whereby works of art are evaluated – characterization, plot, language technique, flash back technique, etc. They sort of x-ray a work of art and actually award credits for these various departments, and on the basis of this say – this is an excellent work of art or poor work of art. I think a real work of art is a very complex thing and the better it is, the more difficult it is for anyone to analyze it. For me the genuine test of a real work of art is the impossibility of analyzing it. I am very sceptical of critics, but they have to make a living. Academically I suppose they are necessary. If you x-ray a work and study it I am sure you look at it in greater depth and you may learn something of the age, of the politics, something of the esthetics and I suppose critics are supposed to point out these things. However, I think ordinary discerning readers can consciously absorb a lot of these things. If you read Dickens you get the spirit of the times.

Q. Critics can take the blood out of a work. I have an idea that books are for people, that novels are to be read by human beings, not merely academicians. I think, throughout the world, academic people tend to believe that books are their property and the property of their students. I find this rather sad.

A. I do also. This is why I tell young writers - just write. Don't worry about the critics. When a reader from India or Australia sends me a letter saying, "I read THE CONCUBINE and I liked it," it's worth five papers from critics praising the novel. That to me is the ultimate satisfaction for the writer.

OLA ROTIMI

Ola Rotimi, the celebrated dramatist, is perhaps best known for his THE GODS ARE NOT TO BLAME. Among his other plays are KURUNMI, OUR HUSBAND HAS GONE MAD AGAIN, OVONRAMWEN and HOLDING TALKS. While I was at the University of Port Harcourt I saw two of his plays performed in Ola's theatre, The Crab – IF and OUR HUSBAND HAS GONE MAD AGAIN. Attending these plays was one of the highlights of my stay in Nigeria.

It was not easy obtaining an interview with Ola as his duties as Dean of the Faculty of Humanities occupied much of his time. Fortunately, we did get together in the afternoon of March 25, 1983 at the Staff Club of the University of Port Harcourt in Choba, Rivers State, Nigeria.

OLA ROTIMI

Q. Ola, I have traveled quite a bit in Africa this year and everywhere I have been - Nigeria, Ivory Coast, Cameroons, Kenya - there is theatre; African plays are being put on everywhere and even in the bookshops here I may have picked up twenty to twenty-five plays, many by dramatists I had never heard of before I came to Nigeria. I have the feeling that drama in Africa is very vibrant. In fact, drama may be the strongest of the literary genres. Do you feel that's so?

A. Well, I feel it's so, but that does not mean the so-called analysts of African literature feel that way. I think they have a warped sense, a colonialist spirit of literary appreciation. They emphasize the novel, then poetry, perhaps the short story and drama is last. This is ironical because in the African tradition, drama is first. The novel is alien. But now, one can catapult oneself from literary obscurity to fame by writing two or three novels. Western critical heritage is so strongly with us that we tend to see the novelist as the leader in literary creativity. One could write six or seven plays and be almost nebulous in the minds of critics. They have a hangover from the colonial sense of literary appreciation that places a premium on the novel, putting drama at the bottom of the literary ladder which is to me misplaced value when it comes to relating it to what obtained in our tradition of artistic expression.

Q. I have noticed plays are put on in villages as well as cities in Africa. It seems that whether critics appreciate it or not, people are going to plays and plays are going to people. In Nigeria various universities have theatre groups. Here you have The Crab. I have seen two of your plays in that theatre. Are these taken out to the countryside?

A. No. Most of them aren't. When I was in Ife I started the University of Ife Theatre and the policy of that theatre was to take theatre to the people and use it as a medium of communication with the people outside the walls of the campus. For eleven years I practicalized this policy. It is on record that that kind of achievement is unprecedented and is yet to be matched by any university theatre in Nigeria. I believe in the idea that writers should articulate concerns of our people and also communicate and share them outside the walls of the university. Writing needn't be done in the English idiom alone. Literacy in Africa is almost negligible. To be part and parcel of the people, writing should also be done in the languages of the people.

Q. Have you written any plays in Yoruba?

A. I transcribed KURUNMI into Yoruba. With the aid of some

Yoruba experts. My knowledge of Yoruba isn't as profound as
I would like it to be. I also, should I say, was instrumen-
tal to the realization of certain plays in Yoruba through a
playwriting workshop which I began in 1973 at Ife and which
went on until 1974. What I tried to do was to introduce potential writers in the traditional linguistic idiom, to play
creation. The kinds of plays that existed were mainly folk
operas (as Ulli Beier refers to them) - suffused with music,
dance, song, etc. To me the illusion of reality can't be obtained in that kind of artistic form. I thought a play
should strive at realism and should have music not solely for
entertainment but to enhance the emotional content of the
play itself. It should try to approximate reality, to establish an illusion of what is happening to man at a given point
in time. So my playwriting course in Yoruba tried to evolve
plays in realistic form and in that way you might say I did
participate (often as a surrogate) in the writing of plays in
the vernacular. These were not my plays. I only instilled
in the students the techniques of playwriting.

Q. Were you ever an actor?

A. I started out as an actor when I was only four years old.

Q. Many playwrights start out as actors. I have thought as an
observer of plays that the critical sense of theatrical
timing would run much easier if one had the immediate experience of feeling that timing as an actor and that that is one
reason why dramatists like Shakespeare, Soyinka, Moliere and
O'Neill succeed. They knew their audiences from their days
as actors. There is a theory in Nigeria that most of the
dramatists are Yoruba because of the tremendous sense of
ritual in Yoruba society and it seems, in fact, that a good
percentage of the plays are by Yorubas. Do you think the
tradition of ritual explains the vibrancy of dramas written
by Yorubas?

A. I don't subscribe to that kind of artistic stereotyping.
People say Yorubas are playwrights and Ibos write novels.
Where do other groups - Hausa, Ijaw, Efik, etc. fit in?
Ritual saliency has nothing to do with this. I think it's
just fortuitous that playwriting and production seem more
pronounced in the Yoruba-speaking sectors of our country.
One reason could be that there was a definite historical development contributing to the fervour of the Yoruba sense of
theatre. You do realize that the capital of Nigeria is sit-
uated in Yorubaland, and that in the nineteenth century
there was tremendous theatrical activity going on there?
For example, Herbert Macaulay, the father of Nigerian politics, was himself an actor as well as an accomplished vio-
linist. All these theatrical sensations spilled over to the
schools, even into the churches, and began a revolution that

13

had an impact on religions in Nigeria. The Cherubim and
Seraphim Church, the Celestial Church of Christ, the Christ
Apostolic Church, all have traditional music as part of their
liturgical proceedings. You might say that at the turn of
the century, Lagos became the center of artistic activity
which mingled Yoruba artistic derivations with those from
Brazil, Europe, Ghana and Sierra Leone. There was a concen-
tration of cultures in Lagos in the late 19th/early 20th cen-
turies. Lagos was the most enlightened center in terms of
Western education. The effect of this amalgam of cultures
resulted in the dominance, you might say, of theatrical performances. The Brazilian "Kareta", for instance, or carnival
dance procession was a spectacle similar to what you might
see in that award-winning film, BLACK ORPHEUS. All these
were happening in nineteenth century/early 20th century
Lagos. This explains the socio-intellectual condition which
must have whetted the appetite of the Yoruba people for theatre.

Q. Has one of your newest plays, IF, been published?

A. It will be in another couple of months. The galleys are
ready.

Q. When I saw IF I was most excited. I don't get a chance to
see that many African plays. I noticed that IF is a part of
what you call a socio-political trilogy. The first work in
this trilogy was OUR HUSBAND HAS GONE MAD AGAIN. It was
written well over a decade before IF. In between you had
written different kinds of plays - historical plays, and
HOLDING TALKS, a modern absurdist drama. Do you want to talk
about this trilogy which obviously is important to you?

A. I describe it as a socio-political trilogy. When I wrote OUR
HUSBAND HAS GONE MAD AGAIN in 1965, Nigeria was under civilian rule. Six years before, I had left home when the transition from British colonial to indigenous rule was coming to
fruition in 1959. You might say, just before the independence of Nigeria, which was in 1960. So I was still imbued
with this awareness of rulership in the hands of Nigerians.
Then I came back in 1966. A new governmental dispensation
had taken over, namely stratocracy, rule by the military.
From '66 to '79 it was military rule. That happened to be a
period when I was also experimenting on a number of levels in
playwriting with a view to discovering some clue to the problem of liaison between a writer who utilizes a foreign language in communication with his people, and his audience.
You might say between '66 and '79 were the years of experimenting on a number of theatrical levels: linguistic, use of
cultural elements, music, dance, mime, sound, etc. I also
tried, in terms of content and theme, to articulate in plays
written between '66 and '79 the anxieties of the present,

14

drawing some hope from the principled nature of the elders of our past who stood in defense of their convictions. You might say that these plays tried to articulate anxieties of the present by illuminating epochs of divisiveness and confrontation of the past. Then came '79 and there was again a change in polity from the military to civilian rule. With the governance of our people back in civilian hands, politics came back into play. My writing focus, you might say, then changed to patent socio-political issues. At that point also my experimentation had begun to take some definite shape and had instilled a measure of confidence into my creativity. I, more or less, reverted to socio-political dramas like their precedent OUR HUSBAND HAS GONE MADE AGAIN which, as I said earlier, was written when my political experience was entirely the pre-independence, and civilian.

I must say that all this isn't a mapped out, programmed modus operandi. I just found myself being impelled instinctively to writing in the veins I did. Perhaps the socio-political circumstances had something to do with the creative preferences. Sociologists would call this the "environmental factor," I guess. For instance, it is rather revealing to see now that the plays that were written in years of military rule deal mainly with warfare: OVONRAMWEN, KARUNMI, AKASSA YOUMI, even THE GODS ARE NOT TO BLAME.

Q. What is AKASSA YOUMI about?

A. It narrates the attack by the Brassmen on the exploitative British trading outpost in Akassa in the 19th century.

Q. Who published it?

A. It's not published yet. I want to write the second part before I get it published. The first part was written in 1977. I am interested in finishing both parts which I see as complimentary.

Q. What is the third play in your trilogy of socio-political plays?

A. WHEN THE DEAD AWAKEN. By the way I use the word "dead" as a pointer to our politico-economic malaise. In that context, we are a dead people. The purpose of the play is to reveal the sordidness of our moribund state in the hope of rousing, of waking ourselves up from it, and heading somewhere.

Q. That's an interesting point. In Kenya people told me "We're a very gentle people and let government walk over us. Nigerians may not be as gentle as us but they're hot and wouldn't stand for the kind of stuff we accept." You seem to say that despite the energy of this country, the dead are still marching.

15

A. "Marching," did you say? That's charitable. Creeping is
more like it. Of course, the dead are still creeping. We
have not yet asserted our individuality as a people. What
have we done to make the outside world respect us as a black
nation? We haven't improved in a way to command the attention and respect of advanced nations. We are still our old
readily exploitable selves. Our economy is not in our hands.
The political tune is dictated by powers outside our territory. We seem so unwilling to take a sane stand. And how
can we, when in finite terms we lack the economic spine?

Q. What about moral spine?

A. How can we talk about moral spine when there's such privation
of human right to better living condition, such insensitivity
by those who claim to be our rulers?

Q. What of all the talk in Nigeria of the "Ethical revolution?"

A. It's part of the gambit to fool the people. I think the Kenyans are flattering us. We're no hotter than they are. My
own feeling is that we are only lucky, and our luck may soon
run out. We're lucky in the sense that the kinds of abso-
lutely power drunk, callous individuals are yet to show their
full exploitative talons on the political scene. And why
this hasn't been so is because we still have as the people's
guardians nationalists like Awolowo,[1] Azikiwe,[2] and Aminu
Kano.[3] These are politicians who committed their lives to
gaining independence for this nation. At the present, they
are not within the circle of those who direct the socio-political destiny of this nation. In other words, they are not
in the NPN (National Party of Nigeria) central government,
and the NPN new breed of politicians seem to be restraining
themselves from total ruthlessness in the exploitation of our
people and liquidation of our resources. The directionless,
self-seeking, wealth-grabbing rulers are yet to do their
worst. For now, they're a bit scared that someone like Azikiwe or Awolowo could make statements to the world press, and
that could crush the very fabric of the rulers' credibility
in the world. My feeling is that those kinds of NPN political moguls are waiting for the demise of these guardians,
these watchdogs. Once that happens, as soon as these men are
eclipsed, either through death or through some political set-
back, you can be sure that those people will show their true
selves and the common man will be doomed forever because
those moguls - as happens in Latin America - will have the
support of reactionary elements in the armed forces to help
perpetuate their stranglehold. It is already happening in
Sierra Leone; has happened in Kenya.

Q. Do you see, after the election, any possibility of an im-

provement in the quality of political leadership in this
land? Is it possible?

A. Yes, it is possible if somebody like Awolowo could be given
a chance. I think Nigeria might have a possibility of wit-
nessing a model kind of government that will set a pattern
for posterity to match or surpass. I say so because Awolowo
has records to show that he is foresighted, result-oriented,
principled and self-disciplined - fundamental attributes for
a leader in our corruption-prone nation.

Q. When you write a play and put on a play, it's a kind of family festival. Your wife is involved. In IF your son, who
was most capable, played an important part. A Rotimi play
is not just an Ola Rotimi play but a family play. Do you
all work together on the plays at home and talk about them?

A. I think it is Aristotle who says every human being or animal
has a mimetic impulse in his nature. For members of my family to have an inclination to acting is nothing peculiar.
Having said that, one might add that perhaps unconsciously
one is perpetuating an African tradition in which the artist
generates his personality not in isolation but as part of a
whole which must start from the home, fanning out to inte-
grate and accommodate society at large. Thirdly, you might
say, in these days of negative distractions, participation
of my kids in theatrical endeavors helps to give them a
sense of positive involvement. I don't call it a recrea-
tional pastime. I see theatre as a serious, almost religious, undertaking and I try to impress upon them the sob-
riety which participation in theatre demands. My wife, on
her part, is a trained singer. We met at Boston University
when we were doing undergraduate work, I in theatre, she in
the school of music. She's always been involved in my plays
- on stage or backstage. Voluntarily. Which is no surprise
since she's a versatile artist, gifted in both music and the
visual arts. This doesn't mean we're the ideal pair in the
world. We're opposites in certain ways, even in art. She's
more finical about details and by far more patient than I
am. I must admit, I'm most impatient for results. Good results of course. She can literally feed on art, whereas I
want to get my art done with and move on to my "eba"![4]

Q. Where do you get your actors?

A. Here in Port Harcourt. I beg, borrow and steal them. I
make use of students too. And, of course, trained actors
from the Arts Council downtown. Finally, I look around for
people who might have the interest. No, it's stronger than
mere interest. It's the impulse, perhaps, to demonstrate
physically an idea before an audience with whom the person
wishes to have an experience. Overall, you might say the

17

paths of recruitment here are long and diverse. In Ife, on the other hand, I had the privilege of being the director of a professional group comprising at least twenty-five regular actors and actresses. Even then, one looked occasionally for supplementation.

Q. You beg, borrow and steal quite a few actors because you usually have big casts. At present you're Dean of the Faculty of Humanities. With all the meetings that you have to attend, with all the time spent on administration and organization, how do you have the energy and time to write?

A. I hardly have the energy to write. Hardly time, either. I think my present position is one that can be described as wastefully irrelevant. Left to me, I would appreciate nothing better than to be left alone to teach, research, write, produce, publish. But then one found oneself in a situation where it seemed there was nobody with the kind of experience in terms of years of service in the university system, and seniority in terms of academic status, to assume the responsibility of Dean when the former Dean abdicated the deanship of this faculty to become Vice-Chancellor of this University. In short, I was more or less conscripted to fill the vacuum. Try as I might, I found myself as one in quicksand, being steadily sucked into the abyss of the post. Candidly, I think it's a disservice to my creativity, productivity and to the nation because when we talk of relevance, I don't think Nigeria will benefit from what I do in the sphere of administration, as compared to what I could contribute in the realm of literary creativity. I want my epitaph to acknowledge the fact simply that I was a writer who used his gift to further the interests of the majority of our people, be drawing attendion of the few who rule their lives to whatever inequities that such rule does perpetrate and perpetuate.

JAMES ENE HENSHAW

James Ene Henshaw is a medical doctor by profession and a playwright by avocation. Although he has been writing comedy since the late 1940's and although I have been teaching African literature for fourteen years, I had never heard of Dr. Henshaw until I came to Nigeria. He is undoubtedly Nigeria's most popular dramatist among secondary school students and is also taught at university level. Among his most noted works are his comedy THIS IS OUR CHANCE and his play on the war ENOUGH IS ENOUGH.

Dr. Henshaw lives in Calabar but also maintains a house in Port Harcourt. When I went to Calabar in December, 1982, I was informed that he was in Port Harcourt. When I returned to Port Harcourt I was told that, in fact, Dr. Henshaw had just left for Calabar. Since it is a three hour journey from Port Harcourt to Calabar, I decided some reconnoitering was in order. Through postal communication and the personal delivery of messages, we succeeded in meeting. The interview took place in Dr. Henshaw's home on March 23, 1983, in Calabar, Cross River State, Nigeria.

JAMES ENE HENSHAW

Q. Dr. Henshaw, I have been teaching African literature for
    fifteen years and I thought I knew a lot about Nigerian wri-
    ting. I came to Nigeria and went to bookstores all over and
    I found your books as available as those of Wole Soyinka and
    Chinua Achebe and yet I had not known of your work in the
    U.S. The first thing I would like to know is something
    about your background.

A. Well, I am a medical practitioner. In fact, I have retired
    from the government service. I qualified as far back as
    1949 at University College, Dublin. I've been in the Civil
    Service most of that time. My family background is quite
    extensive. I am an Efik man and come from the part of Cala-
    bar called Henshaw Town. Henshaw Town people were among the
    founding fathers of Calabar. My own particular family is
    called the Ewa Ekeng family. My great great great grand-
    father was called Ansa Effiom. He was, in fact, the founding
    father - the first born of the founding fathers of the Efik
    of Calabar. It is from "Ansa" that Henshaw, through many
    generations of relationships with Europeans, came to be my
    family name. In the same way the "Effioms" of Calabar be-
    came "Ephraims" later on and the "Akabom" became "Cobham".
    My father was the Honorable Richard H. Henshaw IV, who
    took over as Etubom (King Maker among the Efik) in 1920.
    He had many children of whom I was the youngest. I was
    born on 29 August, 1924. My mother was Princess Suzanna
    Henry Jacob Antigha Cobham, daughter of the Etubom of Cob-
    ham Town of Calabar. It was my senior brother who sponsored
    my education from early childhood.

Q. You have been writing plays for a long time?

A. Yes, even as a medical student. In fact, THIS IS OUR CHANCE
    was written when I was a student in Dublin. It was put on
    by the student union, The Association of Students of African
    Descent at Mespil Hall in Dublin. That was in 1947. I was
    the secretary of the association. Nobody thought of me as a
    writer, but I wrote good minutes so they asked me to write
    up a skeleton of this play and it seemed to work. I had to
    write parts to fit in people who could play. There is a
    part called Aye, a maid of the palace. I had finished wri-
    ting the play with no girls in it, but when a very beautiful
    girl student turned up it wouldn't have been nice not to put
    her in the cast, so I wrote in the part for her. Years
    later, when I was working in Port Harcourt, one afternoon
    there was a knock on the door and it was a Mr. Allan Simms.
    He said he was a representative of the University of London
    Press, and had been going around looking for scripts of
    plays. He wanted something African. People had told him I

20

might have that sort of thing around. By now I had rewritten THIS IS OUR CHANCE and a number of other plays. I rewrote them when I went to graduate school in Cardiff, South Wales. He took them to Britain and I honestly was very surprised to get a letter from the publisher saying this was the kind of thing they wanted. I was still very reluctant because I wrote them for my own personal relaxation and for friends. Until Mr. Simms came I had no idea of having my plays published.

Q. How many plays have you had published?

A. Nine – in five separate books.

Q. Have you produced any of these?

A. No, I have nothing to do with it. I do give little indications, guidelines, for young people.

Q. You mentioned yesterday that you deliberately write your plays for a younger audience. On the other hand, ENOUGH IS ENOUGH is meaty stuff.

A. I didn't write ENOUGH IS ENOUGH for young audiences. I wrote that one for the people. It is about the war, as you know. But you could say I am still thinking of young people, trying to project a positive feeling instead of looking back at the sorrows of the war.

Q. The play is very powerful, especially the recognition scene where mother, father and child come together. It isn't light stuff, although it is comedy. You deal with the whole issue of saboteurs or the idea of saboteurs in the mind of insecure Biafrans.

A. Yes. It predominated the whole war. If somebody pointed at a chap and said "You are a saboteur." it was a very bad thing. You observed in that play I did not mention a word about Biafra. At the time I expected it to be a very lonely view, given there was a lot of emotion on all sides. After the war people could say "Well, we have forgotten about the war." But for the person who has been bombed out of his house or sent his son to die, it's not just a question of forgetting. This was a terrible civil war. In those circumstances I held on to the hope that after some time people would come together again in this country just as we are doing now. People are now talking about the war openly. Chief Ojukwu[5] being back in the country confirms this. Let me tell you a little Efik story. When tortoise was going to market, he was tied up by his enemies. As everyone was going to the market, they passed by Tortoise and saw him being beaten. "Serves him well," everyone said. On their

21

way back Tortoise was still being beaten. They asked "What did he do that he is being beaten from morning to night?" I said that one of these days Ojukwu might come back, and that is what has happened. I think people have genuinely forgotten about the war. I did not actually intend ENOUGH IS ENOUGH to be a comedy, but I always like comedy, because comedy keeps Nigerian audiences from going to sleep.

Q. ENOUGH IS ENOUGH represents a break from what you had done previously. Much of your earlier drama was light and was obviously for entertainment purposes and was rooted in a certain Western idiom. It seems you had an affection for Oscar Wilde and Bernard Shaw. ENOUGH IS ENOUGH is completely Nigerian. Your predilection for clever comic verbal felicity was abandoned in this particular play. It's my theory that the war is too serious a subject to be treated lightly. In your particular case ENOUGH IS ENOUGH comes as a surprise to someone familiar with DINNER FOR PROMOTION or THIS IS OUR CHANCE, although the comic view that you have of people drinking from the same river obviously exists.

A. It is the natural progression, if you like, of the general Nigerian/African philosophy. Left to the village this is what the Nigerian would do: plant, sing, drink together. Unless something happens. But we should not keep eternal enmity.

Q. But if this villager goes to the city he is likely to club someone to get water first.

A. Of course. But I have said a lot about the village setup through many things I have written. One may have a home in town but on the other side of Calabar is what we call "Plantations". You live in the city or town and you have a dacha - village home. You can't say I come from Henshaw Town. It's always - where do you come from in the plantation? I spent my early years in my mother's "plantation", Ikot Ene. Henshaw Town has its own "plantation" too.

Q. What does "Ikot" mean? Many Efik and Ibibio towns have Ikot as part of their name: Ikot Ekpene, Ikot Akpan.

A. The people of or people from.

Q. In this discussion you have talked at length about your Efik roots and some of the ways of the Efik and yet you have not written plays rooted in Efik mythology or thought. Soyinka, on the other hand, is nourished by the Yoruba world, Achebe by his Ibo heritage. Have you ever thought about writing a play about Ekpe society?

A. I've thought about that accusation for years. I have only
touched on Efik culture in the little book called CHILDREN
OF THE GODDESS. The Efik have what they call the Goddess.
Incidentally, the whole Efik nation or tribe of Efiks is
dominated by three forces: First, the Obong of Calabar;
second, the Ekpe secret society or cult; and third, the
Ndem, Goddess of the Efik, who lives in the river. To come
back to the matter of being an Efik and yet not writing
about the Efik apart from CHILDREN OF THE GODDESS, I have
finally succeeded in translating Shakespeare's JULIUS CAESAR
into Efik. It was extremely stimulating. I had to make so
many references – not only transliterations, but I had to
project the story in such a way that if anyone had never
read the play, they would have the feeling of the original.
I have had to dig out a lot of the depth of language and
meaning of the Efik language. Perhaps that is my own con-
tribution to my Efik heritage. One or two people are still
reading the script. It will take a bit of money to publish
it. I think the market is big business and I don't know
how to write for the market.

Q. I think you're being modest. Along with Cyprian Ekwensi and
Amos Tutuola you were writing in the late forties and early
fifties. They have received considerable recognition, yet
you, who are in your own way a pioneer, have not received
comparable critical attention, despite the popularity of
your plays. I wonder why and if you feel this is unjust?

A. I don't think so at all. Writing started as a hobby but
started to lose its hobbiness after some time. I never had
the opportunity to sit down and write except last year. I
never had the opportunity, being a full time doctor. You're
moving all the time. I find my mind is quite relaxed if I
take up a new play with all its characters. It really re-
laxes the mind.

Q. Anyone who has been to Ireland gets theatre in his blood.

A. Ireland certainly helped a lot. We were theatre goers,
rather than cinema goers. I have no reason to complain because I don't usually see those things the critics write. I
do know that some mention is made occasionally. Recently
St. James Press in London, now taken over by MacMillan, com-
piled something about contemporary authors writing in English. I was very surprised and delighted when somebody
posted the book to me with things written about my plays. I
don't know where they got the information. I lack involvement. I don't think I have emotional involvement in the
world of art and theatre like Chinua Achebe or Cyprian Ekwensi. That's their profession. I am a doctor first and
only secondly a writer.

Q. Do you go to the theatre a lot?

A. There's no theatre here except in the university. I went to
see a play last year and enjoyed it.

Q. Do you attend any of the school productions of your plays?

A. I used to love going to those. I used to get courtesy invi-
tations from some parts of Africa. These are the things I
have enjoyed out of this. I have been invited to a number
of productions in the country and enjoyed them. I just
laughed like anybody else. You never know what the producer
is going to do.

Q. There are other African writers who are medical doctors.
Agostinho Neto of Angola was a medical doctor. Lenrie Pet-
ers, the poet from Gambia, is a doctor; Teixeira de Sousa of
Cape Verde is another.

A. And there is a professor at Enugu, Professor Okoro, Professor of Dermatology. He has written some novels. In Port
Harcourt there are two doctors who are classical pianists.
But getting back to ENOUGH IS ENOUGH, the whole thing started with a lot of massacres. I refer to an Efik proverb
about the bird of the night which asks "Why is there fear in
the bush?". Nigerians knew and felt a lot of fear. There
were a lot of massacres in the country.

Q. Nigerian writers are still saying the same thing - enough is
enough: we have had enough corruption, enough political in-
eptitude, enough selfishness. If I can be Biblical, the
writer here is like an Old Testament prophet saying "Beware,
beware." You were doing that in ENOUGH IS ENOUGH. It's not
merely a plea for communion, but a cry that without this
communion the world is an unpleasant place to live in.

A. I agree with you entirely. ENOUGH IS ENOUGH is a call to
end war and come back to brotherhood. Enough of the bad
things, of the confusion. It was a long, terrible period in
this country and I had very close and personal experiences.
We were in Enugu when the first shells landed near Radio
Biafra which was directly across from where we were in the
Ministry of Health. The whole place was shaken up. This
was not the first time I was involved in a war, but in Enugu
it was closer. I left Enugu and came to Uyo. My family was
already there because we knew the next thing the Nigerian
army would do was take Calabar, having taken Bonny. We
didn't want to find the family separated so we kept together
until one morning there was a lot of shooting and the next
day we became Nigerian again. Having grown up at Christ the
King College Onitsha, there were a lot of people I knew -

24

some on one side, others on the other, so that there was always this hope that your friends would come back together.

Q. Were the Efik as resistant to Ibo domination as some of the Ikwerri and Ijaw? When Biafra annexed this territory and said the Efik were Biafran, was there a lot of resistance to amalgamation here?

A. Biafra was a very perfect machine for totalitarian government. If you were a dissenter you dissented in your mind, or within the circle of your closest friends. If it leaked out, you were a saboteur and were put into a camp. It was in everybody's interest to do your work strictly as a doctor. If they were Biafran soldiers, you treated them; if Nigerian - you kept to your trade. What is called domination in this country has taken a political slant almost to the extent of neutralizing itself. It becomes so clear if in one town, for instance, you see Efik or Ikwerre or Ijaw people but the people in power come from another tribe. What I mean is, people thought Ibos dominate this and Yoruba that. I think the grievances people suffer individually are worse than those they suffer collectively. We Efik people here regard ourselves as the Children of Israel. We are a minority. We don't want to dominate anybody. We just want to be left alone; to do our Ekpe. We're not even asking for more than our share of the national cake, just the little part that belongs to us. Politically, all the Efik are asking for is to get a space for the Nigerian sun to touch them when it comes out. All the same, I do not contribute to the idea that Nigerian literature should be a vehicle for the advancement of ethnic prestige. And as far as I know, no author in Nigeria has deliberately gone out of his or her way to do such a thing.

I.N.C. ANIEBO

I.N.C. Aniebo, novelist and story teller, is one of the exciting young writers in Nigeria. Three of his books, two novels and a collection of his short stories, have been published by Heinemann in the African Writers Series.

I.N.C. Aniebo was one of the writers I specifically wanted to interview while I was in Africa. I felt that as a member of the 'second generation', the post Achebe-Munonye-Soyinka-Tutuola generation, he could offer a fresh perspective. Moreover, since Aniebo was trained professionally as a military man and was involved in the War as a soldier, I wanted to hear what he had to say about the War and about the literature of the War.

I.N.C. Aniebo was Dean of Students at the University of Port Harcourt when I was at the university. The interview took place on February 10, 1983, at his academic offices at the University of Port Harcourt in Choba, Rivers State, Nigeria.

I.N.C. ANIEBO

Q. I would like to ask about your background.

A. I was born here in Port Harcourt and went to elementary
    school in the North, secondary school in the East and then
    immediately thereafter joined the army. I was trained in
    Ghana and the U.K. and then sent to the Congo (Zaire) with
    the U.N. peace keeping force. After that I came back to
    Nigeria, and then went to staff college at Fort Leavenworth,
    Kansas. When I came back, about a year later, the Civil War
    broke out and I was in Biafra at the time so I took part in
    that until the end. All of us, who were fairly senior offi-
    cers before the war started, were discharged from the army
    even though the Nigerians gave the impression that they took
    everybody back. I tried my hand at a trade but it didn't
    work. I took off to the U.S. to U.C.L.A. where I did my
    studies.

Q. You're pursuing a degree in history at U.C.L.A. Is that
    correct?

A. Yes. My first degree is in English.

Q. Ojukwu also was in the Congo when you were?

A. Yes - up to 1963.

Q. What impact did the Katanga conflict have on a Nigerian sol-
    dier, i.e. going to another African country and being in-
    volved as a peace keeping force when, in a way, what happen-
    ed in Nigeria in the late sixties turned out to be what had
    happened in the Congo?

A. I can only speak for myself and the people I commanded at
    that time. As you know, the Congo was very underdeveloped.
    There was a clear demarcation between white people and black.
    I went into Manono area in Katanga which is the biggest zinc
    producing area. It has a huge hydro-electric plant which
    served most of the mines. The workers' quarters were like a
    shanty town with a water pump for every six houses, open pit
    latrines, as opposed to white areas where the managers and
    inspectors lived in really posh houses. We had to stay in
    the white area since they had all run away or had been
    killed. The feeling of the Nigerian soldiers was that we
    were more advanced than these people in this kind of demar-
    cation. Most of us felt superior, especially the young of-
    ficers. We felt what was happening in the Congo couldn't
    happen in Nigeria but if it did, it would be worse. I be-
    longed to the Fourth battalion at that time, November 1960.
    The Fifth was led by Ironsi. They went into the Kasai area.

28

We went into Katanga. Ojukwu went to the Fifth Batallion as
a staff officer so he was not really involved in the fighting. I went as a subaltern.

Q. I have done some reading on the war and in a way it seems to
me that the fictional works based on the war should not be
seen totally independently from the historical works on the
war. General Madiebo's THE NIGERIAN REVOLUTION AND THE BIA-
FRAN WAR is extremely well written, extremely lucid. You,
as a novelist and short story writer, are in a relatively
unique position in that you are a trained military man and I
am wondering if you think you have a better opportunity to
understand what happened because of your military knowledge
as well as your literary background?

A. I was in a position to see what happened on the Biafran side.
The people who have written so far, like General Madiebo - I
find his book deceptive although I agree with you that it's
well written. But I think it tells a false story of what
actually happened. He seemed to be keen in putting the blame
on somebody which is not right.

Q. That is also apparent in Frederick Forsyth's biography of
Ojukwu, EMEKA, in which Gowon is painted as the devil and
Ojukwu as a saint. Do you think those writers do that because as military men they see themselves as fighting for
the right cause?

A. No, I don't think so. I think they are biased in favor of
themselves. I don't know if you have read General Olusegun
Obasanjo's MY COMMAND.

Q. I can't find it.

A. Heinemann has it. It was first published by Heinemann of
Nigeria and then Heinemann of London. It's another one-
sided story of how he achieved, how he succeeded. There's a
new book that has come out by Major General Garuba, our former Esternal Affairs Minister, in reply to Madiebo's. But
he too is biased.

Q. Chinua Achebe and John Munonye have said that despite all
the books written on the war, the real story of the war
hasn't been told.

A. I agree.

Q. Well, what of your own novel, THE ANONYMITY OF SACRIFICE?

A. To me that was just a little story that I told at a particular time in my life. You see, I was detained by Ojukwu from
1968 until the end of the war, and I had to keep myself from

despair. They said I was a saboteur, although I had been found not guilty of sabotage by the same tribunal (headed by the late Justice Nkemena) that condemned Banjo, Ifeajuna, and others to the firing squad.

Q. Did you write that book quickly?

A. Yes, in two weeks - three weeks.

Q. I know Angolan writers who were imprisoned during that war. Luandino Vieira wrote various books while he was at Tarrafal Prison. Some were written in only one week. I know this because at the end of his books he lists the starting date and completion date. I imagine he experienced the same kind of compulsion at that time.

A. I wrote a short story a day until they decided they weren't going to shoot me. Then I began a novel.

Q. Are you going to write a major novel on the war?

A. I have about three started. I don't know if I will merge them into one. After I finished ANONYMITY, I started what I call my real novel, and did about one hundred and eighty pages. At the end of the war I lost it. Somebody lifted it. That was the one I was going to publish first. I was going to tell the story of three men from three areas of the East, fighting from Port Harcourt and retreating, and their experiences. It was the fall of Port Harcourt rather than Enugu that broke Biafra's back. Now I don't know whether to write three or four short novels or to write one big one.

Q. Eddir Iroh has written a trilogy. Might you do that?

A. I haven't been able to decide.

Q. If there is a dominant theme in the war literature, it seems to be moral pollution in Nigeria. From my brief stay here I have come to believe that those who died in the war, those who were famous like Christopher Okigbo, or those anonymous village boys who were killed, are still being betrayed by the living. Whatever principles were being fought for on either side, in a moral sense, have not been achieved. In fact, my Nigerian friends say this is a different country since the war and a much less pleasant one.

A. I agree with the last statement that this is a different country and a less pleasant one. But I would hesitate to agree that what was being fought for has been betrayed because even the people who died, except maybe for Christopher, didn't know why they died or what they died for. My feeling is that before one can posit that statement, one has to see how the war affected the village people. Except Chris, but

even in his case there was a certain amount of naivete. I
won't say I was very close to him, but quite close. Just before I left I had joined with him and Chinua Achebe in his
publishing company that he had started and of course it col-
lapsed in the war. We had a series of discussions and at
that time he did express an interest in joining what he called the revolution, that is the battle Biafra was waging
against Nigeria. I told him "Don't be silly. You're not a
trained soldier. You may pick up rudimentaries from certain
exercises, recess, combat drills, assaults, house-to-house
searches and the like; you may pick up those rudimentaries
but you will not really be an asset. You would be the last
person I would like to have in my platoon." He was so excited about it all. He saw it, in my opinion, in a fictional
light. I also questioned whether he knew what he was dying
for. To me, his death was senseless - a waste.

Q. Was the Biafran cause a just cause or was it a fiction created by propogandists?

A. I wouldn't say one way or the other. Initially the cause of
Biafra was good. But I do not think it was worth the number
of lives that were lost and I think at a certain time, maybe
early '68, the people realized it was not worth the number
of lives they were losing. It became more and more difficult
to get young men to fight. All of a sudden we had to begin
drives for recruitment. We had to go into houses and literally drive them out and capture them immediately. As you
moved into the villages most of the young people ran into the
bush to get away. If you had done your groundwork well, you
left another group there to catch them. One of my uncles was
severely beaten when they thought he was hiding one of his
sons and he had to tell them I was one of his sons before
they let him go.

Q. Heinemann is coming out with a collection of your stories.
How many are included?

A. I think about a dozen. I'm not sure. The title is OF WIVES,
TALISMANS, AND THE DEAD.

Q. Let's talk about wives. Wives and girl friends do not fare
well in all your novels and stories. In the story " Sign of
The Times"a woman has an abortion and is almost psychologi-
cally destroyed. In "Shadows" a woman is murdered by her
lover because she is unfaithful to him. And in THE JOURNEY
WITHIN and THE ANONYMITY OF SACRIFICE women are badly treated by men. This appears to be a theme you've been concerned
about since the early 60's.

A. Very much so. I feel in Nigeria the relationship between
male and female hasn't reached the state where you can get a

marriage of minds. The older I get the more I accept this
basic fact and I'm afraid it may never reach this state.
Once in a while I have seen a case where a woman has reached
a mind relationship with a man, but it is someone that she
didn't have an emotional tie with. Where there have been
emotional ties, where some kind of socially accepted habita-
tion has occurred, I find that the woman loses out. It may
be different in Europe and the United States.

Q. A reading of Western literature doesn't indicate that. The
theme of the colonization of women started in the 19th century. Ibsen, Flaubert, Tolstoi and others saw women as social victims. Variations on the theme continue today. It's
interesting and perhaps appropriate that some of the major
African defenders of women, who do it most successfully, are
men. Rene Philombe and Guillaume Oyono-Mbia of Cameroons,
you, Ngugi, all are strong defenders of women and very good
writers as well. I don't understand why French writers such
as Mariama Ba and Aminata Sow Fall are infinitely superior
to those women writers in Nigeria and East Africa who are
writing about the same thing. I don't know why, since Nigeria has produced so many good writers, the women who write
on these subjects don't seem to measure up literarily.

A. I think you have a point there. I find Nigerian women writers not nearly as good as men. My only explanation for this
is that the women haven't been encouraged to go into writing
as much as the men. To me I would say the women are on the
same level as the Nnamdi Azikiwe newspaper era. These were
writers who published poems, wrote works in the 40's and 50's.
I think that's the state women are in at the moment in Nigeria and that they will grow.

Q. You are not the only military man in Nigeria who has turned
to fiction or poetry. Mamman J. Vatsa is a poet. Are there
others?

A. Not poets as such. Ben Gbulie is a novelist. FIGMENTS OF
NOTHING was published by Fourth Dimension. He has also written FOUR MAJORS which is a story of the first coup. I can't
think of any other.

Q. Have you found the transition from military life to academic
life any more peaceful?

A. Let me say my literary life has always been peaceful. I was
writing when I was in the army. For me, literary work is
getting away from everyday existence. Now that I have made
it my life's work, I am not sure I will enjoy it as much.
It's not such a transition. It's just that I shifted.

Q. In African literature one of the dominant elements is the recapturing of African history, Africans telling African stories rather than Europeans telling African stories. These are frequently about historical events and historical figures, i.e. Chaka, Sundiata, Ovonramwen, etc. Do you see it as the function of the artist as well as the function of the historian to retell history to educate the people?

A. I won't say we're actually retelling the history of Africa. I feel that up to now the history of Africa has not been written. It is being written. The classic example is Chinua Achebe's mention of Joyce Cary in MR. JOHNSON in which Cary tried to show that from the master's point of view, the servant might be an idiot who could barely remember things you want him to remember. But when the man went home to his own family there would be another point of view. His children would see him as an autocratic father figure who knew what the white man could do. Achebe tried to show it would be wrong to accept the European role as the truth. The relationship between these disciplines made me leave English and go to history, gathering material for some literary work. I hope that history will be my scholarly side while literature will be my creative side. I am afraid if I went into literature, writing criticism, I would be afraid to create anything.

Q. That could only happen if one swallowed too much academic poison.

A. How do you determine how much? If you want to make it, you have to swallow a certain amount. The people who teach you would have swallowed some of the poison.

Q. What's your opinion of literary criticism of African literature?

A. I don't think there is so far. Unlike English critics, African critics don't encourage writers. Why do African critics wait until some European says "That's a great writer."? Why not zero in? All you find is Chinua Achebe, Wole Soyinka. We have yet to be introduced to exciting new writers. Our critics are afraid to say something about a new writer and are writing about the same people. Some of them go off to Europe. Why does Echeruo have to deal with Joyce Cary? Who cares about him when there are young writers waiting to be talked about! So far African critics haven't changed.

Q. Do you see any social commitment or idealism on the part of African critics?

A. No I don't. European and English critics are not afraid of losing their livelihood and not afraid to explore. I find our critics very timid. As the editor of KIABARA I receive a lot of academic work and it just bores me to death. When I

get a journal like CRITICAL INQUIRY from Chicago or TRI-
QUARTERLY from Northwestern I see the depth of writing that
one enjoys. There are certain revelations - new writers,
not just Hemingway and Faulkner - masters in their own time
but they don't say everything. Achebe wrote his first book
in 1958 when I was in secondary school. I'm surprised to
see new critics still writing about that book. I could
understand if he had continued to produce. Why don't they
write about others like John Munonye? He has written six
books, but you rarely find a critical work on him. If a
critic thinks he's not a good writer, he should tell us why.
I wish African critics would wake up.

JOHN MUNONYE

John Munonye is the author of six novels published in the African Writers Series by Heinemann. I believe that at different times I have taught four or five of them in my African literature classes. I have particular affection for OIL MAN OF OBANGE. In that novel Munonye succeeds in a heroic description of an ordinary man, who sacrifices his own life for the well-being of his children. There are certain lines in Munonye that are so good that when I read them I am aware that he is a veritable poet.

The interview with John Munonye just happened. I was a weekend guest at the home of Chinua Achebe in Ogidi when Bob Wren, an American professor at the University of Houston and the author of a good book on Achebe, appeared. The next day Bob was going to Owerri in the hope of meeting John Munonye in conjunction with research he was doing for a book on the University of Ibadan from 1948-1970. I tagged along and after Bob completed his interview, I spent a half hour talking with Munonye.

The interview took place on January 17, 1983, in the headmaster's office at Government College, Owerri, in Imo State, Nigeria.

35

Q. I had heard that you were retired and after seeing you in
the class today, it is apparent you are not. Would you
please explain this?

A. I was more tired than retired. I moved straight from primary school to secondary school to university and then worked
for twenty-three years. There was no time I could sit down.
At the age of forty-seven I retired voluntarily from the service. I did everything I could do. I worked all over Eastern Nigeria. I taught last year, this year and probably
will teach next year. Then I'll take a long leave.

Q. Other African writers, Ola Rotimi, Chinua Achebe, Wole Soyinka, for instance, are associated with universities. They
teach university students. How do you as a teacher of literature to fourteen and fifteen year old students try to in-
still a love of literature and do you prefer working with
young students?

A. Essentially I am a teacher. I love teaching, whether English
literature, or history. The subject I would like to teach is
Latin. Teaching is my career. My career is in education. I
wanted to get a feel as to what is going on in schools again.
So I am teaching English language here. Getting to your
question, I'm teaching AS YOU LIKE IT now. I tell my students "You'll probably be reading this play later in your education." It's the same with THINGS FALL APART. These are
books they'll read more than once. What's important is to
find out what a book means to a student at this particular
moment. I want to stimulate my students - get them to write
poetry. The sky is blue. Well, write how you feel about it.
I am introducing them to the richness of literature, to the
fact that a writer creates a world of his own.

Q. That's interesting. Baltasar Lopes, the writer from Cape
Verde, chose to spend his teaching career at the secondary
level also. He had university offers but he turned them
down.

A. Great to hear that. The same is true for the contemporary
English novelist, Margaret Drabble.

Q. You were trained in classics and today classics is almost
dead. When I went to school, I had to study Latin, but today
none of my students have studied Latin. Do you find that we
have lost something and gained something less in the abandon-
ment of classics?

A. Let me start from the end of the question. Classics will

36

come back. When you talk about nuclear dismantling, what do you do after that? Classics will come back, if not in such precise structure, in some structure people would like to handle. Maybe Latin literature, maybe classical thoughts.

Q. Do you know Dr. Bernard Fonlon of the University of Yaounde? He too majored in classics. He has related many African political and literary events to Greek and Roman times. He quotes Caesar's "Gallic Wars," Cicero and others.

A. I don't know him. But I too am at home with the classics. It is their simplicity I like, a kind of subtle simplicity.

Q. Is there a Greek or Latin writer of whom you are most fond? You speak of the simplicity of classic writers, and I have noticed that simplicity is a quality you strive for in your writing. Are there any particular tragic writers with whom you feel an affinity?

A. Of yes, Virgil and Homer. The death of Priam in Virgil is masterful. And the death of Ajax in Sophocles - they use such simple words for such great moments.

Q. Your novel OIL MAN OF OBANGE is a kind of classical tragedy in that there is victory in defeat and dignity in striving. The same simplicity you talked about seems to be apparent.

A. You're very right. The death of Jeri's wife was very well handled. She dies and you move on to the next scene.

Q. Eddie Iroh once told me he thought OIL MAN was one of the great African novels.

A. You know, it's not even my favorite book.

Q. Chinua Achebe has alluded to the fact that he especially likes Thomas Hardy, for Hardy knows that tragic stories are more interesting, that stories of people who fail are far more interesting than stories of people who don't fail. And Hardy is very classical. He has a classical sensibility. Is he a writer you have a particular affinity for?

A. You know, to my shame, I didn't read literature at university. Hemingway tenses me up too much. And Joyce I can't get through. But I like Wodehouse and that nineteenth century French writer, the one who wrote GERMINAL. Emile Zola. He writes from out there.

Q. Many of your novels are set in villages. The village, from what I can tell, is a much happier place than cities almost everywhere on this planet. Some writers, you, Elechi Amadi, seem to have maintained your spiritual attachment to that world. I wonder if your humanity as a writer stems from the fact that you have been attached to the village?

A. I don't know about my humanity, but it is a fact that I grew up strongly in the village. Right now I have a home in the village. It is my home. Therefore, it is not surprising that my earlier novels should be located in the village. There was lots of poetry, music; there was humanity in the village. When somebody like Jeri suffered, the community was there. But something terrible has happened. The village is no more. That's tragic. I went back to find my village and it was gone. It is surprising no writer has taken that up. Today it is difficult for me to set a book strictly in the village of OBI.

Q. I see the bridge in "A Bridge to a Wedding" as a metaphor for unifying - unifying families, communities, even traditions. It seems to me that Nigeria is in need of bridge building and that the bridges that were burnt in the war haven't all been repaired in the psyche of the nation. Perhaps that explains why so many writers, good and bad, continue to write about the war. Would you comment?

A. The psyche, the human psyche, takes a long time to repair. Physical and economic wounds are still there. If you are a writer and want to write, you must go back to the war. The war is a natural theme. Everyone wants to have a try at it. I'd like to see someone write on the better side of it. An Igbo girl marries a Yoruba boy, that kind of thing. I don't know any good novel on the war. THE COMBAT by Omotoso was almost good. Now is the time to set down and do a real successful novel on the war. In this country we are in too much of a hurry. We should move slowly. Develop a sense of history. We are all hectic all the time. Let us move slowly.

Q. I live in a village in the United States to escape this sense of hectic pursuit. Wordsworth was talking about this in the beginning of the nineteenth century. "Getting and spending, we lay waste our powers/Little we see in Nature that is ours." Wordsworth saw the movement to cities, the quality of urban life as a sort of pollution. Maybe this problem in Nigeria is a variation of a theme of modern man.

A. Our own case is very different - negatively special. There is never a dull moment. In some cities in the world you can see plays on the weekend. It is an alternative to all this rushing about. In Owerri we haven't done these things. We need theatres and concerts to feed the soul. If they made me governor the first thing I would do would be to establish a special fund for theatre arts. We had a life which was destroyed and we haven't tried to replace it. As an example, you go to a party. The women bring the food and the men give the women drinks. We do this in the village. Why don't we do this in Nigeria? Use tradition intelligently in the modern world. This is a minor example. We should be able as Igbos to do this.

Q. What young Nigerian writers are you most fond of?

A. Omotoso, for one. I wish he wrote more. There is too much effeteness. Not just the new ones, but even the ones who were writing before. What is happening to Nigeria in the Nigerian literary scene? I would advise you to investigate the secondary school system.

Q. Have you ever considered writing plays?

A. No, but a novelist is a playwright, isn't he? It's the same thing; you create characters who speak to you. But you know, we have only produced one great book, Achebe's THINGS FALL APART. Why can't we write like the Russians? That's what I would like to know.

Q. You'd need hundreds of years of suffering.

A. Then we'll suffer.

GABRIEL OKARA

Gabriel Okara is one of the two or three best known African poets who write in English. His volume of poems, THE FISHERMAN'S INVOCATION AND OTHER POEMS has been published by Heinemann in the African Writers Series and by Ethiope Press in Nigeria. Okara has published a novel, THE VOICE, and a collection of children's stories. While in Nigeria I made a special trip to see the River Nun because that river has flowed in my mind since I first read Okara's "The Call of the River Nun."

The interview with Gabriel Okara was more or less arranged by my friend Chidi Maduka who teaches literature at the University of Port Harcourt. Knowing of my interest in doing a series of interviews with African writers, Chidi, on his own initiative, contacted Okara and cleared the bush for an interview. In fact, on the day of the meeting, Chidi drove me to Port Harcourt. The interview took place on February 8, 1983, in Gabriel Okara's office at the Rivers State Council for Art and Culture in Port Harcourt, Rivers State, Nigeria.

GABRIEL OKARA

Q. What do you do here at the Rivers State Council for Art and Culture?

A. I am here as writer-in-residence and I am running a writers' workshop for the Council, a workshop to encourage young writers - not too young writers - anyone at all who is interested in writing and wants to start. I ran the workshop for about a year and then it was suspended because of no money - financial problems. They haven't the money to operate it. So the workshop is suspended for a while, but people still come with their manuscripts, and we talk about them. They even come to my house with manuscripts and so, even though the workshop is suspended as an organized thing, it still continues. I am here as writer-in-residence to encourage young writers or anybody who wants to start writing.

Q. This is interesting because in many countries, including Nigeria, writers are frequently connected with universities and therefore work with students in an academic environment. Do you think you have a better opportunity working on a one-to-one level?

A. I think the advantage this has over university is that this is informal, person to person, chat and talk. I tell my students to forget anything academic. I don't talk about what a stanza is; I don't talk about how a poem gets started; I don't talk about Shakespeare, Milton or any of the contemporaries. Sometimes we do give examples. But my emphasis is cathartic. If you want to learn to swim, you don't stand by the riverside; you jump in. Someone who knows how to swim might say "Raise your right hand and kick your legs." But this is not my way. My task is to encourage and draw out talent in the young writers. Some are very good. At first, I had over one hundred participants, but some fell by the wayside. I ended up with a core of ten who are very fine. Even if it was only five it would be good.

Q. In conjunction with this, I came across AN ADVENTURE TO JUJU ISLAND and noticed you had written other children's books as well. How did you come to write children's literature?

A. I had the idea of writing children's books, but I hadn't come around to doing them before the governor, Melford Okilo, called me and said "I don't want artists to starve. I want artists to live comfortably." That was after they asked me to write children's books.

A. AN ADVENTURE TO JUJU ISLAND obviously has a social warning; it is intended to impress upon young people the danger of

42

drugs. Is there also the same moral concern in the other children's books you have written?

A. Impregnated in all of the stories are some moral values, and traditional values - good ones. Children now-a-days in urban cities are all uprooted from villages and traditions. We have to go back. Take, for example, the tradition of killing of twins. I wrote a story about that. A boy and a girl are called by their father, who tells them the story of Christ, that it was Christ who was responsible for their being alive because the missionaries told us that the killing of twins was bad. Otherwise they would have been killed. Christ says children should be good and obey their parents. The boy and girl go to school and do good work. In the second part of the story some of their former mates became jealous of this boy, who was once like them, and they threatened him. He attended a meeting in the bush and convinced them that they should become good boys too.

Q. I would like to talk about your poetry, in particular, and Nigerian poetry in general. You seem to be, in the most general terms, a poet of nature. In reading your poems in THE FISHERMAN'S INVOCATION as well as in the journal KIABARA, I noticed that the River Nun is your friend. There's somewhat of a spiritual affinity between you and that river and also certain nature imagery recurs. The moon, for instance: "The Moon in the Bucket" and "Cross on the Moon." These images from nature seem to predominate in your poetry. Maybe you would like to comment on your feelings toward the River Nun and birds, stars, trees, water. I am reminded of Wordsworth, but I don't wish to impose a factitious comparison.

A. I grew up in a rural village and in the environment in which I grew up, you see water, and the river is our means of communication. From the river we had our fish; we threw the nets for our daily food, etc. There was a thick forest around the village. We killed animals. Sometimes we went to shoot birds with bows and arrows. Once I went with other children and lay quiet and waited for the birds to come. There was this beautiful bird who came and perched on one of the branches. One child wanted to shoot it, but it was so beautiful I couldn't think of having it killed, so I made a noise and the bird flew off. I used to have those escapades in the bush. Then I read Wordsworth. When I read that poem about birds, I think it is called "Spring", I remembered that bird. And so I grew up in an environment of nature, with the River Nun and the moon. Stories were told in the moonlight and when storytellers came from other villages, the whole community gathered. There were big drums sometimes to dramatize the stories. The moon, the stars, the clouds, the rain - they were part of my environment. So, since any writer or novelist writes from his experiences. I think these things just have to come out in my poems.

Q. One of the qualities of your poetry is a kind of seductive simplicity. It seems that a student in first year university can read your poems and get something out of them or someone like me, can find nourishment as well. There seems to be a debate going on in Nigeria about obscurantism vs. simplicity in poetry. Obviously your predilection is toward the simple. Do you have any sympathy or appreciation of the difficult poetry of say Soyinka or some of the early Okigbo?

A. My own concept of poetry, and probably the origins of poetry, is that it's a communal affair, not one person trying to speak to himself. He wants to communicate, whether he likes it or not he's communicating, by songs, ballads, etc. I feel that since a poet is not just writing for his own personal consumption, he wants to communicate with the reader, to transfer his experience to the reader. When you write a poem in difficult language, I think you are defeating your purpose. So I write naturally. I do not want to outdo the British. Maybe, perhaps, my knowledge of the language is limited, but I feel that if you want people to read your poems and enjoy them without first cracking their brains to see what is there, then you have to write straight forward poetry.

Q. On the other hand, I think there is a kind of mask of simplicity because ultimately your poems are not simple. Ultimately there is some relationship between a particular physical event and a spiritual experience. What I am suggesting is that you use simple language but that does not imply that the experience communicated is simple or shallow. This is a quality of certain poets that I personally happen to like, but I know other people who prefer a journey to the world of the complex.

A. In one of my poems a tree falls in the river through erosion and the water wavers as it rushes by. There is pressure of the water until the tree submerges and the water flows over it. That sort of thing - you can take it literally. The water running over, pushing down the tree. You can also have some deeper meaning. There are two levels of my work.

Q. One of the techniques you seem most happy with is assonance, particularly in conjunction with internal rhyme. There's a pattern, an order created in your free verse primarily through sound. Is this quality an attempt to recapture in writing rhythms of Ijaw or an attempt to create a rythmical essence independent of English and Ijaw?

A. I think it's independent of either. I like music and I play

44

a little piano. So that the music in it is from my knowledge and love for music. That intrudes into what I write.
We are sort of a musical family. My daughter sings.

Q. In your poem "Piano and Drums" which specifically deals with
music, I have thought that when you alluded to the concerto
with its emotional peaks and valleys that you really were
listening to a particularly piece, perhaps the Chaikovsky
piano concerto.

A. I can't remember which one now, but at the time I wrote that
poem, many many years ago, I was listening to a piece of
classical music. Chaikovsky? I'm not sure. I like concertos. They are just like sonnets to me, short and concentra-
ted. Symphonies are more vast. The impact of concertos is
to me more immediate, more personal. So I wrote a poem on
the piano and drum, symbolizing European and African cultures.

Q. In your poetry there seems to be a sense of the marriage of
pain and beauty. Somehow there is born out of pain greater
sensibility, greater compassion, greater humility in a cosmo-
logical sense, greater religiosity. Is this a valid concep-
tion?

A. Yes. When we take the concept of beauty, different people
have different concepts of beauty. We are all trying to see
beauty from different angles. Three blind men are trying to
describe an elephant. One holds a tusk, one the tail, one a
leg. We are all trying to describe what beauty is from different angles. You may find beauty in something that to all
appearances is very very ugly looking. You can see beauty in
pain, in something painful. But there is also beauty in ac-
comodating or uplifting that pain. Beauty is apparent in
times of trial, during difficult situations. These situations bring out the courage of individuals. There is beauty
in courage.

Q. The war was the mother of a lot of literature in Nigeria, but
it seems from my point of view that much more work has been
done in prose than in poetry and this isn't always the case
with war literature. In England, in the first World War,
many good poets were produced. Why do you think that poets
have been less engaged in writing about the war than novelists or dramatists in Nigeria?

A. Let's take myself, for an example. After the war (during the
war I wrote some poems as it was going on), but after that,
in those unsettled times, I lost manuscripts going from place
to place. And then, the experience was so traumatic that
when the war was over and I came back to Port Harcourt, it
was as if you were bottled up in a sort of darkness and sud-

45

denly brought out into light. For the first year or two I couldn't write a word, prose or poetry. I was just blank because of the experiences. That was why some of the poems I had to write two, three, five years after the end of the war. Then things began to come back to me. Probably, as the years go by, more and more poetry will be written. As for me, I am going to write more poems. I am seeing more vividly what happened during the war. I was, however, involved in writing a play during the war. We were a small colony of artists that functioned throughout the war. It was a haven of peace even though fighting was going on around us.

Q. Did you put on that play?

A. We were going to put it on for Ojukwu, but the war ended suddenly and he was gone.

Q. In his introduction to THE FISHERMAN'S INVOCATION, Theo Vincent alludes to a projected work of yours called THE RISE AND FALL OF TORTOISE. Has it been realized?

A. No, not yet. I have to do a lot of work on it. Some of the stories I collected, about one hundred, got lost during the war. The tortoise is a symbol of something used by man to work out his own ideas. When the tortoise was sent a sign that his ideas worked out, he discovered some did not work out, while others worked out well. It took all the intelligence and wisdom away from tortoise, so he was eventually defeated by a goat. There came a time when man realized he didn't have to live by might alone. He had to live by using his brain. The same for tortoise. Tortoise was working in the forest and came to a place where a large tree had fallen across the path. He stood there a long time thinking how to get over that tree. A little child came and said "What are you doing?" He said, "Thinking of a way to get over that tree trunk." The child said, "Don't you see the space between the ground and the tree?" Tortoise thought, "A little child came and taught me how to get across!" He was annoyed. In anger he scattered all his wisdom on all the streets all over the world. That was man's way of retrieving the wisdom given to tortoise. Everybody became wise, and tortoise had no more wisdom afterwards. Even a goat was wiser. I have to do research to see if what I am trying to say is the same in other stories from other lands. I want to relate this to the development of the human mind. You will find different ages throughout civilization, the iron age, the bronze age. I want to see whether these stories can also represent certain stages in the development of the human mind. This is the project I am working on.

Q. The Igbo tell a similar story about Tortoise, "The Calabash of Wisdom."

A. Yes, I know that story.

SAMSON AMALI

Samson Amali, dramatist and poet, often works bilingually in Idoma and in English. This is the case with his two poetic dramas, THE LEADERS and ONUGBO mlOko. Both the spirit and the structure of Samson's work is rooted in Idoma culture. In fact, he has for many years, made a conscious effort to study the oral dramas of his society. By writing bilingually he enables readers from throughout Nigeria to enter the Idoma world.

I had not heard of Samson Amali until one Sunday morning in January. I was bird watching, admiring the squacco herons and lily trotters, with Professor Kay Williamson of the Department of Linguistics and Languages at the University of Port Harcourt. When I commented to Kay that I was interviewing African writers, she mentioned several writers working in indigenous languages, none of whom were familiar to me. That evening she brought to my house four or five books, two of them plays by Samson Amali.

I flew to Jos in the North to interview Samson. We met in his office at the Department of Theatre Arts where he teaches at the University of Jos. For four days Samson escorted me around Jos, showing me the various landscapes of his beautiful city. The interview took place on April 1, 1983, amidst the giant boulders of Shere Hills National Monument, outside of Jos in Plateau State, Nigeria.

SAMSON O.O. AMALI

Q. Samson, you're a young man, yet you have been writing for a long time. Some of your early books of poetry were published in the late 60's. In fact, the books of yours that I was able to get were published in Ibadan from '68 to '72. But after that I haven't been able to find books of yours. What have you been doing since '72?

A. I have been writing. After August 1972 I went to the University of Wisconsin, Madison, U.S.A. for my doctoral degree in Theatre Arts and while I was there, I was writing. I took my Ph.D. in play writing/play creating. I finished that in October 1976. So from '72 to '76 I was writing a lot except that they are not in print because the market people expect to see books in commercial form. What would interest you is that I try to write something every day of my life, so for me it is not a question of stopping to write. Essentially I write at any point - day and night and anywhere.

Q. Yesterday you mentioned that quite a few of your poetic dramas have been put on.

A. Yes, plays like THE DOWNFALL OF OGBUULOKO, ONUGBO mlOko, ADELA, THE FAMINE, etc., have been put on. But before we get into that, let me explain some fundamentals about my writing. I would like to say that research work that I did, that eventually resulted in my Ph.D dissertation and which I have since further worked upon, I am getting ready for publication. It is built on a very ancient African oral drama and literature. In Idoma it is known as Ikpelokwooka; the English equivalent is Inquest Drama. I have found that in the Idoma Society and in many parts of Nigeria and many parts of Africa (I investigated twenty-six African societies), they have inquest drama and literature. In Idoma, inquest means an investigation into what caused the death of a person. In other words, if anybody dies in Idoma society, be he grown up, child, or any human being, there must be an inquest drama to find out what has killed this person. The person, between you and me, might have died of a motor accident or T.B. or small pox. The society recognizes these various forms of illness that could cause death, but the society also recognizes another existent form of illness other than the physical cause, so they are very emphatic about that. Beyond what you and I can see physically, other things are responsible. So when anybody dies there is a drama to re-enact and bring out elements visible and invisible that are responsible for the death of the person. I went to different Nigerian communities and tried to find out why or how this came about. The response I got was

50

that it started with death. We do not know when. Some of
the elders said it came with humanity - with life. The inquest form of drama in Idomaland, to me, is very fundamental
and very important in the study of African literature and
drama. In fact, I am still researching into it. It seems
everything in life is centered around it. It's another dimension to human existence. If you're not careful you will
not know it; it just passes you by. I found it also existed
in Europe and the United States, but there it takes different
forms. I found that the one that exists in the U.S. was
brought in by the British during the early colonizing of America in the name of the coroner's inquest. That's the form
it has taken now. But in Africa inquest drama is a major literature. You can get hundreds and thousands of people in
the audience. In the inquest play the life of the person is
dramatized. If you had a dream about the person there is a
point in time where it is dramatized.

Q. Who puts on this drama?

A. It is the entire society. This leads to the structure of
African society. If you take where I come from, traditionally, you have various lineages. I used to think there were
three in my district, but I found well over twenty-six lineages, each descending through a particular father in the re-
mote past, for seven or eight generations. These form a community. Within that community they dramatize inquests. So
when a person in the community dies, there will be about
10,000 in that community and each lineage sends representa-
tives to the inquest, to perform the inquest drama. Things
they had never thought of before come out in the presence of
these societal collective dramas. Nearly every group within
the society plays a role. The inquest is a collective societal drama. The entire society creates the drama. This is
distinct from the plays I write, where I sit down and write
alone. The inquest has a collective authorship. I hear people say, "We haven't read anything of yours since '72." Certain things take a long time to mature. As I said earlier, I
have been writing and I cannot stop writing.

Q. One of your early plays, ONUGBO mlOko, seems to be an inquest
play.

A. I wrote that before '72. But I would like to believe I have
known more about inquests since then. A large part of the
play is inquest where the elders meet to discuss what has
caused the death of Oko. What has been done in this study is
to study an indigenous African oral dramatic form which the
people have been practising before Islam or Christianity
came into this part of the world. Because if you have read
some literature on this subject, you know people tell you
that Africans had no drama and no literature. But for cen-

51

turies there has existed what I have now called "oral drama."
Plays are created orally, preserved in the brains and when
the time comes, people create them orally. My doctoral the-
sis is divided into three parts: 1) a production, literary
technical study of how the inquest drama is put together; 2)
the oral inquest drama itself as the entire community per-
forms it. The scripts are there. I translated it into English; 3) Having done that, I took the forms of Ikpelokwooka
Inquest and used the forms to create a play from a myth about
an Idoma woman, Odegwudegwu. This woman is part of the ancient tradition that women don't see ancestral spirits at
burial, but somehow this woman saw the nakedness of the an-
cestors. The penalty for that is a live burial. This woman
is to be buried alive. They dig a grave to bury her alive.
She walks around it three times led by three men; her eyes
are blindfolded. The first walk around the grave is accom-
panied by a solemn song, with almost two thousand people present. Her father bids her farewell. In the second walk her
husband bids her farewell. He can't help her. The third and
last solemn walk begins. She stops just before she enters
the grave, and at that point her children emerge. Something
happens. The society is turned upside down, for never before
have children been present in such circumstances. A second
later she would have been in the grave. From that point on
the elders restrain her burial. A divine oracle is consulted
and ancesters offer sacrifices and say that from then on no
man or woman is to be buried alive. Since then it's never
happened.

Q. When is this?

A. It's a myth in Idomaland. This myth is chanted by the ances-
    tral spirits any time they perform in public. What I did
    then was to take this myth, which was changed by the ances-
    tors, and use the inquest forms and structures to dramatize
    it. So the play grew from the indigenous inquest forms.
    When Shakespeare was writing he was taking some English or
    European oral traditions and using them superbly in his own
    ways. But he did not present these from the point of view of
    the people but rather from his own point of view. I guess
    different ages have their own different styles of doing
    things. What I am trying to do, and encourage others to do,
    is, if you are an American or a Nigerian - observe the socie-
    ty and give us the collective, individual and societal dramas
    that are there, first. The societies have their dramas. How
    do we use them as playwrights?

Q. There are other Nigerian playwrights who go back to tradition-
    al sources.

A. Yes. Just like I took ODEGWUDEGWU and dramatized it, Wole
    Soyinka, J.P. Clark, Ola Rotimi, S. Oti, Kola Ogunmola, Zulu

Sofola, Duro Ladipo, Wale Ogunyemi, Meki Nzewi, Ene Henshaw, etc.,have done the same thing. J.P. Clark, I think, in OZIDI, is the first major Nigerian playwright who really took a whole traditional form of drama and gave it to us. He recorded it on tapes in the field in Ijaw language, transcribed the Ijaw and translated it into English and presented it to us on sound film. He also made records of the oral performance. Then he wrote, purely in English, the OZIDI play based on the OZIDI SAGA. Where I differ from Clark is that I create my plays in both Idoma and English. Clark creates his plays purely in English. I am writing in two languages. My first play THE DOWNFALL OF OGBUULOKO was in 1964 when I was in high school. It's out of print now. I wrote some scenes of this play in Idoma, Pidgin and English.

Q. Are these plays that you have written in Idoma put on in the schools here in Plateau State or Benue State where the Idoma people live?

A. Yes. I have requests in Jos to produce them in May but because my students will be having exams I don't think it will be possible. ONUGBO mlOko was read in Idoma to Idoma elders when I first wrote it. It's been performed in English because of the composite nature of the members of the audience. But the Idoma people are asking for it in Idoma. There's the problem of training actors and actresses in the language. Bilingual area of creativity is an area which I have been in since 1964. I believe that I should create my plays in Idoma and English at the same time.

Q. Is there a problem getting these works published?

A. Yes. There is a major problem of getting such works published. Every effort has been almost single-handed on my part. I have worked with Professor Robert Armstrong, formerly the Director of the Institute of African Studies at the University of Ibadan - now professor at the University of Nigeria, Nsukka, for a long time, and we are still working together on many Nigerian cultural and literary projects. He specializes essentially on Idoma culture. Getting publishers is very frustrating. There are over one million Idoma people, so publishers claim the market is not much. They say they want a wider market. They want to make plenty of money. This is the argument you get. They will tell me that my plays are excellent, but they can't help me. Alternatively, they will say, "Write only in English and then we'll publish it." So that problem exists. I know and I have articles in my possession written in English about my plays, poetry and other artistic works in Idoma and English which are very positive indeed. Take a play like ONUGBO mlOko, which is in in Idoma and English and which is very popular in Idomaland

and in Nigerian Theatre and which is a very important dramatic piece. This play and THE LEADERS were first published
in Idoma and English as part of the special publications of
the Institute of African Studies, University of Ibadan. Now
these editions of the play are exhausted and I want to re-
publish them. I am their author and I have the copyrights.
But each publisher I have approached said that though the
plays are excellent, he would not be able to publish them in
Idoma and English, bilingually, and that he would publish
only the English versions. I know that the future of the
dramas and the literatures of the nearly 450 different but
deeply related ethnic groups and languages in Nigeria lies
heavily in the proper development of the plays, poetry, novels, stories, etc., in these Nigerian languages and in English. I am not deterred!

Q. It's a kind of colonial spirit?

A. Yes. That's what it is. In fact, at Calabar the paper I
presented was on "Why I write my plays in Idoma and English."
We must print things in our own languages for the future.

Q. Can't the writers who choose to write in African languages
band together and create communal pressure?

A. As of now, I think I am the one championing the cause. There
are Nigerians who write purely in Nigerian languages and
don't want to take the trouble of making the same work available in English. The way I create, I do it simultaneously,
Idoma and English, thereby making the work available in both
languages at the same time. I could create in any other Nigerian language, for example, in Yoruba, Hausa, Igbo, Kan-
uri, Fulfulde, Nupe, Igala, Igbirra, Edo, Tiv, Efik, Ibibio,
Ijaw, Urhobo, etc., etc., if I knew the language well. I
don't discriminate against language. But I am more at home
with the two languages Idoma and English.

Q. You have made some records?

A. Yes. These records contain indigenous oral dramatic performances. Don't forget - what is called oral literature in
Africa is actually oral drama. If you talk about Yoruba
ORIKI or Igbo MMONWU or Hausa BORI or Tiv KWAGHIR or Igala
OGANI, any of these, what it is in essence is oral drama performed before your eyes. I went into the villages and studied oral inquest, music, ancestral stories and folktale performances. I put them on tapes and edited them. I preserved
the performances in record form instead of book form. To get
one record done takes months and years of research, artistic
and academic hard work. I think now we have about thirteen
of these different performances. When people talk about publishing they don't talk about that. I tell you, the trouble

54

we had, we were ostracized from the community. They said we had revealed this very secret oral drama which should not be touched by making records out of it. But now everyone is happy that this has been done. Small children, adolescents the the grown ups in Idoma-Otukpo now use the records to learn the sacred songs, drama and rituals of their land. The demand for the records is quite high.

Q. The same sort of thing happened among the Ojibwe Amerindians in Ontario in Canada. A painter named Norval Morrisseau painted secret symbols of his people, secret myths, and he was ostracized for revealing them to the white man. But now this painter is one of the most praised artists in Canada. He has opened a new direction in Canadian painting and has various followers from different Amerindian communities.

A. When the first records came out, they were taken to the village for the elders to hear. They said they must not be released. That those were secret funeral songs and chants. Each time a person dies most of these twenty-one songs are performed just before the corpse is buried. These records are now almost the savior of the society. When people die now they go and collect the records.

Q. When my wife and I were guests at Chinua Achebe's in Ogidi a record was being played at a neighbor's home for a funeral all through the night and Chinua commented that this is a continuation of oral tradition, but a modern variation.

A. These records are modern in the sense that the performers are like you and me. They are so important now to the community. The elders feel apologetic toward me and Armstrong They now think we were doing the right thing.

Q. I have interviewed six or seven Nigerian writers. Several of them have a similar complaint, "Critics don't pay enough attention to us." The kind of work you're doing does not get much attention. What about the African critics, those who talk about colonialization of the mind and the arrogance of western critics. Why aren't the Nigerian critics paying attention to their writers?

A. Exactly. I see what you mean. It's what we discuss all the time in the class. I don't know.

Q. Is it because these critics have become unconsciously Westernized?

A. That's part of it. I had a problem at Ibadan. I read English for my first degree. I got honors in English. During the course of this I talked to the head of the department. I asked him when I was going to be taught the literature of Nigeria. I said I had been there two and one half years and all I had been taught was the literature of Britain. I asked when I was going to study the real literature of Nigeria, the literature I grew up in my village knowing. I said I had been reading the literature of England all through - Shakespeare, Keats, Shelley, and I love them, I do. Since I have some degree of artistic interest I identify with them. But what of our own? He said, "Mr. Amali, the question is not appropriate. You should master these first." Essentially Nigerian departments of English, even today, are heavily loaded with this approach to the study of English.

Q. But Nigerian students today do read Chinua Achebe, Wole Soyinka, John Munonye. When I was teaching at Port Harcourt I found students were very familiar with those Nigerian writers published by Heinemann.

A. You can understand that. There's the money business and a certain literary orientation. We discussed this in Calabar. All those writers fall into the same class. Other's don't belong. We want to say something new. With me, when I first wrote and wanted to publish my first selected poems in 1968, I sent twelve to an internationally known publisher. He said he had read them and they were beautiful. He asked that they be changed so they could be used in secondary school. He said that I would be known all over the place. I thought about it and I talked to my friends who said I would make money. Then my mind tells me - is it the money, what's more important? Is it the idea? And I kept my poems as they were and published them myself.

Q. Since the world is paradox, you are both a poet rooted in Idoma and at the same time a poet who goes far beyond the geographic and psychological borders of Nigeria and Africa. You have written poems in French, you have written odes about American astronauts and you have written poems celebrating integration - of time, of nations, of man and animals. Many Nigerians claim that a writer must be political in contemporary Africa. Unless he is political he is not fulfilling his responsibility to his society. Your commitment seems to be in several directions, not just to Idoma, but to people in general.

A. I think I agree with you there because the creative force to me knows no boundaries, no limitation if you really have it. It's not something that you can just limit to a particular dimension. You can control it somewhat, but if it's truly organic to your nature, you find life within life itself - in everything, within the conscious and unconscious, the seen and the unseen. I react to the moment. In THE LEADERS I think I would like to modestly claim that I have made an attempt to weld the Nigerian nation together - a genuine attempt for the first time, I believe. It's a reaction to these political, historical developments people are talking about. One's interests are many, very very many.

Q. America has not come off very favorably in the eyes of some Nigerian writers. J.P. Clark's AMERICA THEIR AMERICA is a vitriolic portrait of America. Some poems I have read by different poets are not very favorable. In CAN NIGERIA SURVIVE? Arthur Nwankwo paints America and Europe as the devil in a morality play. Yet you have a certain affection for my land. When you speak in your poems of another man named Armstrong, you see him as an emblem of what is best in man.

A. That's correct. Personally speaking, Amali speaking, all human beings, regardless of their color or shape, are essentially the same whether Nigerian or American. Nigerians feel pain and Americans feel pain - live, rejoice. Once you go beyond the artificial boundaries that surround humanity you can breach the barrier of the shallowness of man and if you do breach that barrier, you will rejoice in the progress of your fellow man, regardless of where he comes from. I think that Nigeria as a nation has problems, moral and material problems. America is a nation with moral and material problems. There are good things in Nigeria and there are good things in America. It depends on what one is looking for. Nigerians are very hard working people. I don't buy the idea that we are lazy. We are not. I have found Americans to be very hard working human beings. They work around the clock and I am impressed by that. The space achievement of the U.S., honestly speaking from the bottom of my heart, I respect it and I respect America. If it has been achieved by any other nation, say China or Russia, I would have the same admiration. That's because the Americans who did that are human beings like you and me and I believe in rejoicing in the achievements of my fellow human beings because that achievement is also mine. The guys who labored in the NASA space lab, they are human beings and I respect them. Maybe they will also respect me if they read a poem or play of mine.

GRACE OGOT

Grace Ogot, the founding Chairman of the Writers' Association of Kenya, and a former delegate to the General Assembly of the United Nations, is a highly regarded novelist and short story writer. Her novel THE PROMISED LAND, first published in 1966, is one of the pioneering works in modern East African literature.

I was fortunate to get an interview with Grace Ogot. When I arrived in Nairobi I learned that she had just left for Kisumu in the West, and that she was due to return the very day I was to leave Kenya. Through her husband, a noted historian in his own right, arrangements were made for an interview on the one convenient day. I met Grace Ogot outside the New Stanley Hotel on Kimathi Street. From there we went across the street to her second storey office of the Jack and Jill Clothing Store that she manages. The interview took place in her office on March 19, 1983 in Nairobi, Kenya.

GRACE OGOT

Q. You have just come back from your home in Kisumu. Your husband mentioned to me that you are currently writing a book
set in and around Kisumu. In your first novel, THE PROMISED
LAND, the lake is part of the landscape as it is in some of
your short stories. Kisumu and Lake Victoria seem to be a
spiritual home.

A. Well, it looks like it because my background and my roots are
around the lake region. The reason I returned there was that
the chap who is doing my first editing wanted me to be around
in case of any language difficulty since he does not speak my
language, Luo. The title of the book coming out soon is
SIMBI NYAIMA. It is simply a story, an historical novel, of
a village of my people.

Q. In Kenya acclaimed writers are writing both in English as
well as their African languages. Ngugi is one. You are
another. This phenomenon does not seem that common in some
other African countries.

A. Although I had always done broadcasts in Luo and Kiswahili as
well as English, there had always been an underlying desire
to write in my language, so that it could be read by all my
people. Only a small percentage of our people speak English.
I felt it the writer's duty to communicate with those who do
not speak English. When I wrote THE GRADUATE my mother looked at the book and said "If only you could write in Luo you
would serve your people well." I thought that challenging so
I did the first Luo novel MIAHA. We translated it and made
it into a play. We took it all over, starting in Nairobi.
We took it to Kindu Bay. The response was startling in that
the older generation were moved to tears. They could see before them their cultural heritage – how people dressed in ol-
den days. Their pleasures and hopes all were evident in this
play. It stimulated their thoughts. It is my hope that people can have proper respect for their own language and will
learn it so that it will not be lost and swallowed up by English and Kiswahili. That gave me encouragement to work on
the second novel, SIMBI NYAIMA, which will be published in
April.

Q. Women in Africa know your work, teach your work, and see you
as one of the early and continuing advocates of justice for
women in Kenya and in Africa. You also have a genuine commitment to the history of the Luo people and as well, a
greater commitment to Kenya, to the spirit of "Harambee".
When you write do you set out to present a specific point of
view? Look at THE GRADUATE. There are certain themes that

60

are apparent - the idea of women who fought alongside the men during the resistance and when independence came were not rewarded as they should have been.

A. First of all, I would like to say that although I am a woman writer I don't set out to write as a woman. I never set out to write that way. I feel a writer should be honest and faithful to the characters whether they be men or women. I set out to write as a universal writer for both sexes. But of course one must see one's society as it is. Sometimes you find a situation as in THE GRADUATE where women in one way or another find themselves in subordinate positions. This does not only apply to Africa. Often there are men sitting on the board who will be interviewing candidates and the job goes to a man even if a woman may be more qualified. In Kenya, for instance in THE GRADUATE, you have seen struggle - what women did and yet they did not get the posts they were supposed to get. In the beginning when men went for elections, women organized the polls. Men in Kenya have never accepted the fact that many women are bread winners. There are single and widowed women who take employment. A second problem is that the Kenyan woman still wants to take a lower position to her husband, who is the head of the family. Considering she has that feeling, the men will always think that way. They will always think they should be given the responsible positions. I do feel we have given men a lot of support as mothers and men have forgotton to give credit where it should be given. In THE GRADUATE, a woman is given a place in the cabinet only because of the death of the former minister when she should have got the job in the first place. This is just one area where women could be given equal chances which they have earned.

Q. Some people equate East African literature with Ngugi. In fact, in certain bookstores in Nairobi, he is the only African writer whose books are available. Many critics write on Ngugi to the exclusion of other Kenyan writers. I am curious what impact this has on young writers. Do they feel that they have to imitate Ngugi?

A. Not really. I think at one time when we held a seminar on children's literature a theory came up that writing is like many branches of life and that we have to stimulate writing in this country. Ngugi dwells on struggle, struggle for this and struggle for that. Then you get writers like David Maillu whom I think is a great writer. He will write the type of novel that forces you to keep your mind on that book until the end. He writes well on aspects that many of us are very scared to write about - about sex - and makes it easy for many people to read. You have others like Meja Mwangi who takes another aspect, and Charles Mangua who is very different. Then you have the type of writing I am interested in

61

that explores family relations. There are other writers like Pamela Kola and Asenath Odaga who are writing children's books. I could mention others, like my son David, who writes for secondary schools from form one to form six. This is another kind of writing. Each takes areas where he thinks he can contribute most. Writing is inspired from within the writer and this inspiration keeps you awake. I feel that we're all inspired to write our own books. From the core of varied literary experiences we bring out our cultural heritage. At one time Ngugi's books may be very popular because at that particular time that kind of subject is current. At one time Maillu may be very popular. At one time p'Bitek's poetry may be very popular. The kind of family stories like my "Wayward Father" reached many hearts in Kenya, even within the church.

Q. Are you familiar with John Munonye of Nigeria who writes stories of families?

A. I haven't read many of his works. Family stories move me a lot and I am a great believer in the family unit. That is where everything begins.

Q. Are there many publishing companies in Kenya? Is it difficult for a young writer to get started?

A. It is. Although we have quite a number of publishing houses in Kenya, more than half of them are foreign owned. In several others the government has some shares, but most shares are foreign owned. We have a few publishing houses like East Africa Publishing House which is indigenous and quite a number of smaller publishing houses. But whether foreign or partly government owned, they are very shy to take up the work of young writers who have not been published before unless the work is perfect, which often is difficult for a beginning writer. So quite a number of works remain unpublished because publishers are overloaded with manuscripts of already recognized writers or are just too busy to give their attention. So today Kenya has quite a number of unpublished manuscripts which could turn out to be very worthy if given the opportunity.

Q. I have been in Nairobi about a week and I notice there is a play being put on by Efua Sutherland of Ghana and that there are several Western plays as well. You mentioned earlier that your play was taken into the country and performed there. Is there much Kenyan theatre put on for Kenyan people or is drama mostly imported?

A. In years gone by such a situation existed where foreign authors were produced, but for the last two years there has been endless drama, not only in the National Theatre but in many small theatres all over the country, written by Kenyans for Kenyan audiences. Hence, the awareness of Kenyan people to patronize something of their own background. Over the last two years there have been many indigenous groups producing local drama either by themselves or from other African countries - not only in Nairobi but also in the countryside. It is an even greater boost that his excellency, our beloved President, has suggested that communities should have cultural festivals annually in languages the people can understand. This will give a big boost to dramatists. I have just been told that Kenya is forming a committee that will start drama for the communities. This will stimulate writing drama. The Minister of Social Services is going to budget funds to enable drama to be put on in mother tongues. Young people will dramatize any book they can get their hands on. Hence my son is dramatizing a very ambitious book of mine of over four hundred pages entitled IN THE BEGINNING. It's the story of my people from the year 97 A.D. The novel will probably be published at the end of this year. It starts with the first settlement and tells how they moved from one settlement to another. My son Michael has adapted this into a play and it will be put on 23 March. If successful, it will be translated for the benefit of the people who need it most. I think drama has suddenly bloomed in Kenya and many parts of East Africa.

Q. I have been in Kenya for twenty-two days. This is a very pleasant environment. As a tourist I can't think of a more agreeable or beautiful land and I've been in many countries. I have friends in Africa who live in societies that don't look very agreeable on the outside at all and yet they say "We're better off than Kenya. Our writers stay. There's no freedom in Kenya." Is this a valid criticism?

A. I think a writer writes about a society in which he lives. I believe that very strongly. I cannot write about any other country. I write about Kenya because it is my people. I have written travelogues. The bulk of my writing is about my people. There comes a time in a writer's life when some of the things he's writing about may not be popular. You know it when you start writing. When you take pen and paper to write you know some of the things you write will not be popular. So if our writers have been in that particular situation today maybe tomorrow it will be someone else's turn. I don't think this is an unusual situation found only in Kenya. It has happened to writers all over the world.

Q. You're abviously a very versatile woman. You've been a nurse, worked at the United Nations, worked for an international airline and now you are running this clothing store. How did you get into the clothing business?

63

A. The clothing store came to my hand by accident in 1967. A friend was recalled home. She had run the store for ten years. I wasn't well at that time and had been off airline work. My friend didn't want to sell the store to someone who would ruin it. I had never done anything like that. I can't even sew. Giving it to me would be the surest way of ruining it. She came a third and a fourth time, tying tight the de-department store around my neck, or as we say in Luo "Otweyo waehno e nguta." That's how I acquired it. There was a small one. Then the government gave me another store and another lady offered me a third one. Because of my writing commitment, I had to give two to other ladies because I wanted to give more time to the big book called IN THE BEGINNING. So I am keeping only this one and I have ladies who are looking after it.

Q. You obviously are interested in historical background. Your husband is a prominent historian. Do you feel that the two of you are paddling a similar canoe and that there is a shared mission of education albeit from different directions?

A. I think Bethwell Alan Ogot has been one of the inspiring factors in my life in that he first motivated me to write poetry which I could not do. Then I turned to short stories. He enjoyed history like poetry or a novel. His books are like works of fiction. He is an African historian writing about people I love which nurses my roots. I would have been a fool if I did not seize the opportunity to use the vast knowledge he has of the background of my people and the way he has assembled everything that has ever been written about them. This has been a great inspiring factor. Through him I discovered that my people have a very great history: long ago they lived on the dry lands of Sudan; I learned of the kingdoms they founded, how they tamed the land and also, through him, I was inspired to go back to my roots and do a lot of historical research. In future this will be valuable for our children, who thought only the White Man had a history and that African peoples had no history. That's why I have pushed my novel back to where we have early evidence of Luo settlements - around the year 98-103 A.D. It has taken me ten years to do the novel. So having been married to an historian has really inspired me.

Q. Will there be a Luo version of IN THE BEGINNING?

A. Oh yes. The Luo title is KAR CHAKRUOK. I think the book comes out better in the language people speak. We have to develop the language and in developing it, it has to have a literature so people can say they read in that language. We must make our people literate in Luo. There is a very great problem of illiteracy. We hope all Kenyans will be literate by 1985. It is our duty to adult literate Kenyans to have works of literature in their mother tongue, not just books on how to plant onions.

AMINATA SOW FALL

Aminata Sow Fall is the acclaimed Senegalese writer, author of three novels, LE REVENANT, LA GREVE DES BATTU and most recently, L'APPEL DES ARENES. Her second novel has been translated into English under the title THE BEGGARS' STRIKE. In the many bookstores of Dakar, her novels, along with those of Sembene Ousmane and the poetry of Senghor, are the most visibly displayed African works.

I went to Senegal in the hope of talking with Aminata Sow Fall. And fortune smiled on me. Through her publisher, Nouvelles Editions Africaines, I was able to contact her to set up a meeting. The interview took place in the late afternoon of April 15, 1983, in her office at the Centre d'Etude des Civilizations, a division of the Ministry of Culture, in Dakar, Senegal.

AMINATA SOW FALL

Q. Aminata Sow Fall, one of your books, LA GREVE DES BATTU (The Beggars' Strike) has been translated into English. Your two other novels, LE REVENANT (The Resurrected) and L'APPEL DES ARENES (The Call of the Arena) have yet to be translated. Can you tell me a little about your background - your education, where you were born, things like that?

A. Yes. I was born in St. Louis in the North, the former capital of Senegal, in a family that was quite well off. My childhood was without problems. I completed my primary and secondary schooling and then went to Dakar where I passed my baccalaureate. I left St. Louis because my older sister had married and had just come to live in Dakar and my mother asked me to go with her to keep her company. Later I went to Paris because I wanted to become an interpreter. I did my studies in Interpreting and in Letters at the Sorbonne. But in the meantime I got married and realized that it would be too difficult to study simultaneously Interpreting and Letters.

Q. As a writer, you express sympathy for the victims of society, those who have bad luck in life. These victims in general fall into two categories - the poor, those who can't fight openly because they don't have any money, and women in modern society. Do you believe that the situation of these two classes of victims can actually improve? There are other Senegalese writers: Mariama Ba who writes about the situation of women and Sembene Ousmane who speaks of the plight of the poor. With all this writing, is there in Senegal a genuine consciousness of these problems?

A. Yes, I believe that it is possible to make society aware of the plight of these victims. Because it is the society that has nurtured these victims. If one looks at my novel LA GREVE DES BATTU, for example, one can see that society itself has encouraged the mass of beggars in its own interest. I think this has not been done deliberately, for the position of the beggar is ambiguous. He is someone who demands money and often the rest of society naturally has a tendency to look down on him. It is not a comfortable situation to beg. And when one gives to a beggar, often he gives merely to get rid of him, so he won't bother him. In our society it is important to understand the nature of giving. One should give purely, gratuitously. That is what should be. But unfortunately one doesn't give freely in our society. One gives because he expects something in return for his generosity. So that an act that should be completely generous is, in fact, dictated by self-interest. Once society becomes more aware of its own conduct, it will have a greater understanding and respect for the plight of the poor, and there will be an improvement in conditions of the poor.

Q. I have visited five African countries this year and have seen several large cities - Nairobi, Lagos, Yaounde. Dakar has many more beggars than other African cities that I know, perhaps because Dakar is a Moslem city and begging is viewed more sympathetically in a Moslem community than in a Christian one. Yet despite the spate of beggars in Dakar, I have the impression that Senegalese writers really love the city. When African writers write about Accra or Lagos or Kinshasa, they recreate an urban hell filled with ugliness and pollution, both moral and physical. Yet here in Dakar, despite the fact that there is more visible poverty, the writers celebrate the city.

A. Yes, Senegalese writers love Dakar; it is normal since Dakar is part of Senegal. There is visible poverty caused by the presence of beggars. That shouldn't be a justification of scorn, for in a general sense we are not a rich people; we have for a long time walked hand in hand with the poor, with poverty. I think what has changed over a period of time, from before the colonial era to the present time, is the attitude of the people towards the poor. The poor have always existed, but one didn't see them in such large numbers in Dakar. With colonization and independence there was a rupture with traditional structure. The poor left the villages and came to the cities where they thought there would be greater opportunities, which in actuality was not the case; they ended up living on the streets. Before colonizaiton, poverty was common. The countries of the Sahel have never been rich, but there existed a sense of solidarity, a sense that people cared for one another, helped one another. People were not as selfish as they are today. Perhaps today we are selfish without really wanting to be, but the structure of the modern world forces us to be selfish. When one has, for example, a small apartment, with three rooms, and one has children and relatives living there, one can't accommodate them. In the past, it was possible. Not too long ago you could see more than fifty people living together in a large house. Today that doesn't happen.

Q. What has happened to the sense of shame? In traditional village societies, there existed a strong sense of community. If one offended the community, the spirit of the community, there was a sense of communal shame. Nowadays, money is king and it seems to me that in nearly all African countries the sense of shame has begun to wither, to disappear. It is more important to be rich than good.

A. That is a problem that preoccupies us a great deal. This is

perhaps why I have focused on the fate of victims, for the
fate of these victims is determined to a large extent by
society's excessive valuing of material goods. There has
been, in effect, a certain degredation in some of our concepts of civilization, and among these concepts is the sense
of honor. A sense of shame used to be something to avoid.
We were afraid of shame. There is a Wolof proverb that af-
firms "It is better to die than to know shame." People have
been known to commit suicide because of a scandal that caused
them shame. Today, because of material goods, because of
money, people have lost their sense of shame or scandal.
Certain people think that money itself can erase shame. That
never used to be the case. This has resulted, I believe, because we have lost much of our traditional education. There
used to be invested in the individual both a responsibility
to his village, as well as a sense of honor. Now one comes
to Dakar, makes his scandal, and there are no communal eyes
to watch him.

Q. I am a teacher. What is a teacher in this world? One cannot
be a teacher of books as something separate from life ifself.
I have often asked myself - What is education? It is not
merely going to university, studying chemistry, physics,
mathematics or literature and then graduating a moral savage.
I consider this a universal problem nowadays; education used
to be rooted in morality, in the spiritual elevation of man
to give of himself to others. Education today is far removed
from the spiritual life of man on earth. You deal with this
in L'APPEL DES ARENES, which, for me at least, can be seen as
a lyric essay on education.

A. Yes, you are right. This is a problem I think about a great
deal. We must give education its original meaning. Education, for me, is synonymous with culture. Culture elevates
man to a certain perspective that distinguishes him from animals. Only man has culture; only man has moral precepts.
Society used to be very much aware of this. It was necessary
to cultivate man as one cultivates the soil in order to enable him to get the best out of himself, to eliminate his be-
stial qualities, his evil, etc. I believe in earlier times
society had this perception of man, and this was made mani-
fest in traditional education. A man isn't merely an object
who is there, who eats, who drinks, but someone physically
and spiritually committed to the betterment of society. He
should act in the highest possible manner. He is not an isolated individual; he is a member of society. I think that
this idea has become lost. The societies that are the most
threatened are those where the break between individual and
society is most perceptible. The more man is isolated, the
more man is left to himself, the easier it is for him to lose
his humanity and be dominated by his animal nature.

70

Q. Women in transitional society are not praised in your novels. Nor are they praised in the two novels of your compatriot Mariama Ba. It seems to me that in the modern world, you advocate a return to traditional wisdom, yet within this transitional world, women have not had equal opportunities to develop themselves fully.

A. That is a very difficult problem. The day before yesterday I read in the newspaper LE SOLEIL a piece by Saliou Kandji. He writes about the travels of Emil Batuta. Batuta wrote about what he saw in a particular African village. What was most shocking was his report of the freedom of the African woman, the respect accorded her by the men. It seemed as if the women, in fact, ran the society. That may be a remnant of the matriarchal system that existed in Africa. Then came Islamization, and with it the false interpretation of certain precepts, interpretations which led to the maltreatment of women. Let me give you an example - the problem of polygamy. Nowadays we talk a lot about polygamy. In the Coran it states that a man may have more than one wife if he will treat each one in exactly the same way. That is a criterion that is impossible to satisfy. From the point of view of sentiment, no man can treat two women equally. And human nature being what it is, the Coran is interpreted in the way that best suits the interests of many men. That is why there are these interpretations that place the African woman in a secondary status. This results more from personal than true religious or social conviction.

Q. African women throughout the continent write about the colonization of women by men. Is the situation of the Islamic woman really different from that of African women in non-Islamic societies? On the surface the situation appears to be the same; women do not have equal opportunity to develop their potential.

A. This is not an absolute verity. In the text that I just cited the author states that when Islam was first introduced into Senegal, it brought with it certain precepts from the Arab world which were not disadvantageous to women. These Islamic precepts were oriented towards liberating women. In Africa at that time women were already enjoying much freedom. I believe that Islamic women are not as subjugated as some claim. They are not more subjugated than Western women. Women who are writing a lot now about the situation of women have been influenced strongly by the West. I personally do not believe that the condition of women is as pitiable as they claim. It is the women who make decisions in society. All familial ceremonies and those that perpetuate tradition are determined by women. Men, even the present government, fight against the estravagent waste of money in familial ceremonies. But

71

no one can stop it because it is the women who are doing this. In fact, if the women could direct their genius towards a positive action, you would not see women, but super-women. I believe the problem of the situation of women is very complex. When one looks at it from a distance, one sees one thing, but when one sees from within, the situation is different. The government has passed a law controlling the expense of familial ceremonies, but to no avail.

Q. Senegalese women perhaps have a certain power because of their beauty. One thing I have noticed in your novels is the cult of the boubou - the colors, the manner of wearing the headcloth - you describe these in great detail. I am reminded of the description of the Kimonas in the tales of the Japanese writer Kawabata. Clothing becomes a work of art and an expression of the good taste or the bad taste of the person wearing it. In your novels I have been struck by the attention you give the boubou; I very much like to look at the boubous; in fact, I bought one for myself in Ivory Coast. Is my perception a correct one?

A. It is exactly right. I don't know the Japanese writer; unfortunately I haven't read any Japanese literature, but the perception is correct. The boubou is a work of art. But it is deeper than that. It is a work of art manifested through external beauty; it is an expression of the good taste of he or she who wears the clothing. You notice that it is not just the women who are well dressed. The men wear boubous as well. A man considers it important to take care in his appearance; he must dress well. He is an elevated creature. This is part of one's culture, of one's taste, of one's spiritual life. It's bad form for a refined, cultivated, good person to dress sloppily. It's bad taste. Even the poor often buy attractive boubous. If I just go out to cross the street, I must be well dressed, for I don't know whom I may meet. It is necessary that each time I am seen I should appear in the best possible state. So you see, there is that profound dimension to all this.

Q. Let me change the subject. Is there a written literature in Wolof and is it being published? Are stories, plays, being published in Wolof?

A. No. But we are beginning, bit by bit, to see literature in national languages, not only Wolof but Diola, Sereer, Pular, Soninke, Malinke. Occasionally pieces do appear in magazines.

Q. When I read Senegalese books I frequently come across words that are not French. Are they Arabic?

A. No, they're Wolof. At any rate, in my case they're Wolof.

I use Wolof expressions; that does not affect the understanding of the text. If you cut them from the text, you still have the same meaning. Only these Wolof expressions enrich the text for one who knows Wolof.

Q. In Anglophone African countries, a lot of work is being done in indigenous languages. Novels, plays, poems are written in these languages. Moreover, some writers who first made their reputations in English have chosen to write in indigenous languages so that literature can be made accessible to those who live in the villages. I have the impression here in Senegal that that is not happening.

A. There is a problem facing publishers. There is not a sufficient market for them to publish in indigenous languages. Les Nouvelles Editions Africaines here in Dakar publishes in French because the local market is so small. In Nigeria, on the other hand, there is a far vaster market.

Q. Sembene Ousmane has made films so that he can reach more people. How successful has that been? Are films taken into the villages? Are many people seeing these films?

A. Perhaps they're not shown in villages, but they are shown in all the movie houses; certainly the films have increased the size of his audience. Motion pictures enable those who do not read to have access to books, to grasp the message of the book. I think that is very important.

Q. Are films being made of books by other Senegalese writers?

A. THE REVENANT is being made into a film, but it hasn't been completed yet and I don't know when it will be completed.

Q. Books published by Les Novelles Editions Africaines are of high quality. But I've noticed that they are quite expensive, especially for one who doesn't have much money. Isn't this a serious problem? Books should not be a luxury.

A. It is a problem, but the publishing houses can't afford to lose money.

Q. In Kenya books are quite inexpensive, while those published in Nigeria are costly. In Cameroon the prices are in between. One thing I noticed here is the accessibility of African books. African books receive as much if not more publicity than French books. For instance, your novels are displayed in the windows of many bookstores. This is not true in other Francophone countries I have visited - Ivory Coast, Cameroon - where one must hunt in obscure corners of bookstores to find African books. In those countries one would think he was in a French bookstore.

A.   Yes, here there has been for some time now a real politique
de livres, to get people to read. Since Les Nouvelles Editions Africaines came into being, this book consciousness
has taken off. Previously nearly all the books taught in
schools were Western and frequently people weren't so interested in these, because the cultural context was not their
own. Now it's good. Recently a Book Day was organized, the
26th of March. Many people attended.

Q.   In the Anglophone countries there were writers of substance
before the 1950's. But with the publication of THINGS FALL
APART there followed an eruption of literary activity.
Chinua Achebe gave confidence to African writers that they
could tell Africa's own story and at the same time do so as
artists of high quality. I am wondering if L'ENFANT NOIR
played the same role for Francophone African writers as
THINGS FALL APART did for Anglophone novelists?

A.   I can only speak for myself, and in my case I've always been
interested in literature. When I was a young student, reading was my only distraction. My father had a substantial
library.

Q.   What did your father do?

A.   He was a high official in the Treasury in St. Louis. So I
spent my childhood reading. I read everything I could.
Even as a student I wrote an occasional poem or sketch of a
theatrical piece. I spent my secondary school and university years reading French authors. The baccalaureate here was
exactly the same as in France. The program was the same;
the examinations the same. When I was at the Sorbonne, I
worked on French authors - Baudelaire, Flaubert, Balzac, etc.
- so that in actuality I was hardly familiar with African
literature. I did read a little, some Senghor, and I remember reading very quickly L'ENFANT NOIR. But when I returned
here to Dakar, I told myself that literature must evolve.
It is very good that Senghor and other writers sought to rehabilitate the black man. To write works on negritude -
that's a good thing. It was a necessary historical movement. But what bothered me a bit was that after Senghor,
writers felt a need to define themselves in relationship to
the West. I told myself - we know French literature well;
the French don't have to explain themselves all the time.
Why do we always feel the need to explain ourselves? A literature is the expression of the soul of a people. I told
myself - I will try to write a novel in which will be ex-
pressed our way of living, our way of perceiving the world
and also our way of criticizing our culture. That's how I
came to write my first book. We should paint, as is the
case with other societies, our own self-portrait.

74

Q. When one reads critical works, there are perhaps three or
   four novelists who always attract attention - Mongo Beti,
   Camara Laye, Sembene Ousmane, Cheikh Hamidou Kane. These
   are the first generation of novelists. Are the new writers
   like Mariama Ba, like yourself, given sufficient critical
   attention? And do you think that your generation is doing
   different things from the generation of Cheikh Hamidou Kane?

A. Yes, certainly we are doing something different. It's a
   matter of preoccupations that nourish a book, because man
   always lives under particular circumstances; he lives a particular moment. Senghor lived Negritude. He lived a moment
   when it was right to rehabilitate the black man, his culture,
   his beauty, etc. Cheikh Hamidou Kane wrote at a different
   moment, when African intellectuals became conscious of being
   torn between different cultures. In that moment he wrote
   L'ADVENTURE AMBIGUE. The generation of today came into being after independence. There are many things to reveal in
   our society and there are many things to sing about as well.
   I believe that is the concern of contemporary writers. After all a writer can't write about what he does not know.
   He describes what he lives. I think society has evolved
   since the time of Senghor, since the time of Cheikh Hamidou
   Kane. Certainly the problems posed by them still exist,
   perhaps to a different extent, so that their works continue
   to have value.

Q. There are many French people here in Senegal. Are there
   French people who consider themselves more Senegalese than
   French? And if yes, does the possibility exist for the em-
   ergence of white writers who express what it is to be Senegalese? For example, this situation exists in Angola where
   white writers, some even born in Portugal, went to Angola,
   acquired an Angolan identity, an Angolan heart. They were
   sent to prison during the struggle for independence. These
   white writers are African writers, Angolan writers. Is
   there a possibility that such a thing could exist here in
   Senegal?

A. I can't really say if there are French people who consider
   themselves Senegalese. But as for their existence as Senegalese writers, that has not yet come about. Perhaps it
   might happen. It depends on the degree of their absorption
   into Senegalese culture. I believe such a thing is possible,
   but it is very difficult. A literature is, after all, the
   expression of a culture, the expression of an experience.
   The Angolan situation is a little different because it was a
   country in crisis, struggling for a common cause and in such
   a case of struggle against an enemy, there is greater national identity. In Senghor's time, when he was at the
   front, when he fought for France, he wrote poems that any
   other Frenchman might have written. It depends on themes.

If one is speaking about a poem of combat, it's not so difficult, but as for a profound reflection on a culture, that's
quite different.

NKULNGUI MEFANA

Nkulngui Mefana is the author of LE SECRET DE LA SOURCE, a collection of tales of the Beti people of Southeastern Cameroon.

The interview with Mefana was a result of circumstances and spontaneity. While I was in the bookstore of Editions CLE in search of literary works by Africans who write in French, my guide suggested I buy LE SECRET DE LA SOURCE. When I asked who the author was, my guide smiled and affirmed that, in fact, he was the author. Of course I gladly bought his book.

It was at this moment that I got the idea to do an interview, for I wanted to know what was happening in Cameroon letters. So, without any preparation, this interview, the first I did in Africa, took place on December 30, 1982, in Mefana's office at Editions CLE in Yaounde, Cameroon.

NKULNGUI MEFANA

Q. Would you please tell me something about your background?

A. My real name is Owono Protais-Aloys. Nkulngui Mefana is my
   literary name. I was born on the eleventh of November,
   1939, in Nkolakomo (Oyeng) in the district of Mbalmayo in
   the Central South. I attended Catholic schools, first at
   the Catholic mission at Obout and later in the seminaries
   at Mvaa and Okono.

Q. What books have you written?

A. Only one of my books has been published to date - LE SECRET
   DE LA SOURCE, (The Secret of the Source), a collection of
   Beti tales. I've tried to render the flavor of the Beti
   world in the French language. I have also written some unpublished works, a volume of poems entitled LA COUPE DE
   LARMES (Goblet of Tears), a novel, LA FIN D'UN MONSTRE (The
   End of a Monster) and ITINERAIRE D'UNE CULTURE OU SURVOL DE
   LA LITTERATURE ORALE BETI (Itinerary of a Culture or Sketch
   of Oral Literature of the Beti). THE SECRET OF THE SOURCE
   is to be translated into English by an American professor
   who visited here, but I can't recall his name.

Q. A majority of recognized Cameroon writers are Beti. Mongo
   Beti, Ferdinand Oyono, Guillaume Oyono-Mbia, Rene Philombe
   - they are all Beti. What explains the predominance of
   the Beti in literature?

A. You are correct. In the first place there was a great emphasis on schooling in the Central Southern part of the
   country. I would also say that the Beti are by nature
   more imaginative than practical. They prefer the humanities - in fact, they practice the humanities. Thus one
   finds many Beti journalists, writers, administrators, law-
   yers, and very few in sciences and commerce.

Q. Is there a "new generation" of Cameroon writers? Certainly the anti-colonial satires of Mongo Beti and Ferdinand
   Oyono were set in earlier times.

A. Yes, the present generation is concerned primarily with
   the moralization, consciousness raising and sense of responsibility of Cameroon man.

Q. What do you mean by "consciousness raising?"

A. That is to say that Cameroon man in the twentieth century must master his historic, social, cultural and religious context. The rupture with our traditions demands that we remodel our personality, and it is to that end that the new generation is committed. Many writers, like politicians, scientists, and others are involved in this task. This is what I mean by mastering our development.

Q. Who are the outstanding young Cameroon writers? Francis Bebey is well known. Is there a single dominant writer under thirty in Cameroon?

A. No. There is no single figure. But Joseph Kenghi and Naha Desire are two popular writers. Kenghi's play DANS LE PETRIN (In a Fix) is particularly popular. It has been successfully staged on several occasions in Yaounde. Desire is a young novelist. His autobiographical novels SUR LE CHEMIN DU SUICIDE (On the Road to Suicide) and LE DESTIN A FRAPPE TROP FORT (Destiny has Struck too Hard) are good. Of course, Guillaume Oyono-Mbia is a major figure in Cameroon letters. His play TROIS PRETENDANTS...UN MARI (Three Suitors...One Husband) has had many editions.

Q. Is Francis Bebey Beti?

A. No, he is Douala.

Q. I have noticed in bookstores of Douala and Yaounde, books by French writers rather than African writers dominate. In fact, one has to hunt to find African books in some bookstores. What is the implication of this French cultural dominance in light of your earlier statement about consciousness raising?

A. I must say that this is more a matter of commerce than culture. Booksellers of this sort are nothing more than business men. Because the French were here for a long time during the colonization of former Eastern Cameroon, tastes in reading reflect this.

Q. The situation is different in Nigerian bookstores where most of the books are African. How do you explain this from a point of view of commerce?

A. In certain countries colonized by the English, writers quickly mastered the language. Moreover, in the Francophone colonies, publishing for a long time was in the hands of French publishing houses. The majority of poets, of Francophone writers, were first published in France.

Q. THE SECRET OF THE SOURCE - is there a principal source, someone who told you stories when you were a boy? Or is THE SOURCE the entire community of elders?

A. Actually the title of THE SECRET OF THE SOURCE comes from one of the stories translated in the collection. It doesn't refer to a particular person.

Q. In Cameroon today is one aware of recently published works by Cameroon exiles living in France? I'm thinking of Mongo Beti.

A. Since a book is a product, one must make sure that those who read it are not intoxicated either from a political or a cultural point of view.

Q. What is your work at Editions CLE?

A. I am in charge of the business and management end of this bookstore, which is a leading seller of books published by CLE.

MANUEL LOPES

Manuel Lopes has been an outstanding painter of the Cape Verdean landscape since the 1930's when he helped to found the literary journal CLARIDADE. His two novels CHUVA BRABA and OS FLAGELADOS DO VENTO LESTE and his collection of stories O GALO CANTOU NA BAIA constitute an essential part of the foundation of modern Cape Verdean prose. Manuel Lopes has also authored two volumes of poetry.

I met Manuel Lopes in his home not far from the Rossio in Lisbon, Portugal. When I arrived I was greeted by a vigorous man whom I assumed to be the son or some other relative of the writer. After all, Manuel Lopes was born in 1907. The man before me looked no older than fifty. After chatting for a few moments with my host and waiting for Manuel Lopes to appear, I dared to ask "Are you Manuel Lopes?" I had been speaking to the author all along. Before returning to the United States, Manuel and his wife were kind enough to spoil my wife and me with a dinner of duck, rice and vinho verde, a Portuguese wine that I enjoy. The actual interview took place on the afternoon of May 19, 1983.

MANUEL LOPES

Q. In the 30's you were one of the founders of the Cape Verdean
    journal CLARIDADE. Along with Jorge Barbosa and Baltasar
    Lopes, you launched one of the early manifestations of Afri-
    can consciousness. And CLARIDADE continued to be published
    until the 1960's.

A. Yes, it was an African, but more specifically, a regional
    consciousness. Jorge Barbosa did not come from the same is-
    land as Baltasar Lopes and I. There were other contributors
    as well - Joao Lopes, who wrote sociological essays and Man-
    uel Velosa. He stimulated all of us, although he wasn't a
    literary contributor.

Q. Who is Manuel Velosa?

A. Manuel Velosa is dead now. He was a journalist, a very cul-
    tured man. He was a merchant as well.

Q. Whose idea was it to establish CLARIDADE?

A. It's very difficult to say. Cape Verde has had a substantial
    literary tradition. Since the 19th century there have been
    outstanding journalists. But journalism is often the enemy
    of great prose. Before CLARIDADE there were other serious
    efforts. Cape Verde is an archipelago and it frequently hap-
    pened that educated civil servants were transferred from one
    island to another or to Portugal, and this resulted in in-
    terruption in the flow of ideas. But in 1936 CLARIDADE was
    born. It expressed the habits, the character of Cape Verde.
    It expressed the life of Cape Verde without foreign importa-
    tion. At that time literature in Portugal was at a low ebb.
    It was not a literature that served as an inspiration for us.
    There was the Portuguese journal PRESENCA, but truly this
    journal said nothing to us. It was, however, a formal revo-
    lution that interested me, but apart from formal elements,
    there was nothing for us. The Cape Verdean after all had his
    own character different from that of Portugal. In certain
    aspects our character is close to that of the Brazilians.
    Cape Verdeans, for instance, suffer repeatedly from droughts;
    in Brazil there is a zone in the northeast that knows fre-
    quent droughts. We read with great attention Brazilian wri-
    ters - Gilberto Freyre, Jorge Amado, Jose Lins do Rego, and
    others, but we never sought to copy the Brazilians. They
    gave us a model of how to do something. This enabled us to
    discover ourselves. CLARIDADE was a self-discovery. Why af-
    ter all is Cape Verde different from Guine-Bissau or Angola?
    One must look at history. Cape Verde was discovered in 1460.
    The first men to arrive there were Antonio da Nola, the Geno-

82

vese, and Diego Gomes. They were of the famous School of
Sagres [6] that produced so many discoveries and explorers under the leadership of the Infante Don Henrique (Henry the
Navigator). Antonio da Nola became the first "Capitao-Mor"
of Cape Verde, the first representative of the Portuguese
government. There was a shortage of manpower in Portugal so
slaves were brought to Cape Verde. The slaves were seized
from the West African coast - from Senegal, from Guine, from
Gambia, from Guine-Conakry, from Sierra Leone. These slaves
were brought in small groups. As a result, slaves were
brought together who did not know each other's language. In
Guine-Bissau alone there are at least twenty languages. Who
solved the problem of a Guinean language? It was the Cape
Verdean who invented "Crioulo" and later exported it to
Guine. In Guine they speak the crioulo of the island of Sao
Tiago in Cape Verde. When the slaves from West Africa arrived at Cape Verde, they found a different ambiance. It
was not easy to find food. There were no forests; instead
of rivers there were rivulets. There were no houses; in
Cape Verde they found the cool northeast wind. They found a
confusion of languages. They found other Africans who spoke
languages they did not understand. In almost every aspect
they found a different world from the one they had known on
the African continent. So "Crioulo" was created. When the
African arrived in Cape Verde his tradition was left behind
on the beaches of Africa. The Cape Verdean was obliged to
create a new system. The Cape Verdean has his own music,
his own dances, his own cooking.

Q. Do you believe that Cape Verde in a sense is similar to
    other islands, in particular Madeira and the Acores?

A. Yes, Cape Verde is certainly more akin to Madeira than to
    Africa or any other country. Cape Verdean culture, Cape
    Verdean civilization, accompanied European civilization.
    One important element in the shaping of a culture was the
    poverty of the islands. The poverty of the islands deter-
    mined the following: The Portuguese preferred Brazil and
    Angola or India. As a result, Cape Verde developed more or
    less on its own. However, it was Europe through Portugal
    that ultimately shaped our culture as it did in Madeira.
    The difference lies in the fact that in Cape Verde there
    were many more slaves, many more blacks than in Madeira.
    This resulted in the creation of a mulatto society in Cape
    Verde. According to the Englishman Archibald Lyle, in his
    book BLACK AND WHITE MAKE BROWN, Cape Verde is neither Afri-
    ca nor Europe. It is much more like the Antilles.

Q. It would be interesting to study similar literary elements
    in Caribbean and Cape Verdean writing. For instance, there
    are distinct parallels between your novel CHUVA BRAVA (Tor-
    rential Rains) and IN THE CASTLE OF MY SKIN by George Lam-

ming of Barbados. There is a character in his book, a Mr. Slime, who gets rich off the people just like Joao Joana. And in each case, the people put their trust and faith in the hands of one who will choke them. Also the theme of emigration, which is so predominant in Cape Verdean prose, appears not only in Lamming's work but in the works by Sam Selvon of Jamaica and Derek Walcott of Saint Lucia in the Windward Islands. I think that islands throughout the world share a fraternal soul. The literature of Ireland has distinct similarities with the literature of Cape Verde and the literature of the Caribbean. Island people are often poor and are torn between the desire to stay and the need to find work in foreign lands. During the famine in Ireland in the mid 19th century, hundreds of thousands of Irish migrated to North America. Economic conditions dictated their leaving Ireland just as in Cape Verde. There are some Cape Verdean writers, however, who see Cape Verde as an African country, whose history is rooted firmly in the history of Africa. I'm thinking of the Nova Geracao, the so-called "New Generation" of writers of the fifties and sixties - Gabriel Mariano, Ovidio Martins, Onesimo Silveira.

A. That's absurd. This is one of the elements of the PAIGC, one of the myths. Cape Verde is not the same as Guine-Bissau. In the first place, Cape Verde is primarily Catholic. Cape Verdean culture and civilization are Western. It has little in common with the various ethnic cultures of Africa. It's like Madeira or the Acores. The great difference is color. In North America the Acoreans segregated themselves from Cape Verdeans. When a Cape Verdean declared he was Portuguese, the Acorians were furious; to them the Cape Verdean is African. The fact that Cape Verde has its own unique culture meant that it was not so difficult to create a Cape Verdean literature. The Cape Verdean travels a great deal. You find Cape Verdeans throughout the world. In Timor there are Cape Verdeans; Dakar has a Cape Verdean colony of 40,000. Mozambique, Angola too. There are more Cape Verdeans outside Cape Verde than inside the country. In America alone there are about as many Cape Verdeans as in Cape Verde. In modern times the most important Cape Verdean emigration has been to Holland. This began in the 1960's. Today they dance the morna, the coladeira in Holland. I spent a week in Rotterdam. It was delightful. There are Cape Verdean hotels, Cape Verdean restaurants, Cape Verdean cabarets. They express their political opinions openly; over 90% of them are opposed to the PAIGC: they want democracy and liberty. In America there has not been such an active political response because of certain fear. Here in Portugal, the Cape Verdean colony has been most important since the last century. The first Cape Verdean became an American citizen in 1834 in the island of Nantucket. From the end of the 18th century Cape Verdeans were whaling off the North American coast. Most of these men

84

men came from the islands of Brava and Sao Nicolau. The men left Brava and went to sea. They went everywhere.

Q. The major Cape Verdean novels, your CHUVA BRAVA AND OS FLAGE-LADOS DO VENTO LESTE (Victims of the East Wind) and Baltasar Lopes' CHIQUINHO are rooted in realism.

A. Yes. Neo-realism developed in Cape Verde three or four years before it did in Portugal. In Portugal it was primarily a political, a social movement, opposed to the dictatorship of the time. In our case, we depicted the life of the people in a colloquial, direct style. I feel an affinity with the American writers John Steinbeck and Erskine Caldwell. I do not think realism and politics go well together. Political concern puts blinders on a writer. It can make him one dimensional.

Q. I'd like to talk about the question of a racially mixed Cape Verdean society. A friend of mine who knows Cape Verde personally and who is of Cape Verdean descent remarked that on the coast the people are light skinned while in the interior the people are black. On the other hand, I have Cape Verdean friends who speak of an absence of a consciousness of color in Cape Verde. I could not find out for myself because I was denied a visa to visit Cape Verde from Dakar.

A. Cape Verde has ten islands. One of them, Santa Lucia, is un-inhabited. Maybe a fisherman here, or a man with his goats there. One island that is distinctly different is Sao Tiago, whose capital is Praia. Praia is a bureaucratic city, the center of government. It appears like a fortress. In the interior (Sao Tiago is a very large island, larger than Madeira or any island in the Acores), there are people who have no contact with the coast. They have their own habits, their own agriculture. These people are black; there was practically no miscegenation there. They aren't "African" though. They don't speak an African language; they don't have African art; they developed their own Cape Verdean customs. The Portuguese government paid little attention to them. These Cape Verdeans in the interior of Sao Tiago are called "Badius". In all of the other islands, Brava, Fogo, etc., there was no such isolation. After 1971, the Badius began to have contact with other people. In fact, some have come to Portugal to take the place of Portuguese laborers who left to emigrate to France. With increased contact and travels, they will change. It is possible that in the interior of Sao Tiago there existed preconceptions based on race. But not in the other islands. There is less racial consciousness in Cape Verde than in Brazil. In America, however, Cape Verdeans have learned to become aware of racial preconception.

Q. In the United States in the 19th century it was far easier for a light skinned Cape Verdean to immigrate than it was for a dark skinned Cape Verdean. For that reason the shippers deliberately chose light skinned Cape Verdean workers.

A. Yes, from the island of Brava. When I visited Providence I met many people from Brava.

Q. You are mulatto?

A. Yes, I am. My father came from Coimbra. Everyone in Cape Verde is mulatto. Even the white man is mulatto. He has a mulatto soul. I came from Sao Vicente. There was and is no racial compartmentalization there.

Q. Your books have been translated into Russian and Ukrainian.

A. Elena Riausova translated CHUVA BRAVA into Russian and Victor Shovkun translated both my novels into Ukranian.

Q. Yet, up to this point, your work hasn't been translated into English. The Soviets seem more aware of Lusophone African writers than do we Americans.

A. I'm still hopeful. A Frenchman from Nimes asked permission to translate OS FLAGELADOS and of course, I agreed.

Q. Do you consider yourself an African writer?

A. A Cape Verdean writer. The African element in Cape Verde did not develop. (Manuel Lopes has an African statue on a table to his right). You see this statue? It is not Cape Verdean. It's from Mozambique. Cape Verdeans do not create African works of art. The closest contact we had with Africa was Dakar, but Dakar was a French center; it was known as "Petit Paris." The Cape Verdeans who went to Angola went as civil servants; they did not bring back an African essence.

Q. Cape Verde has produced an astounding number of poets. In Manuel Ferreira's anthology NO REINO DE CALIBAN (In the Kingdom of Caliban) there are hundred pages of Cape Verdean poems. And his book is merely a selection of representative poems.

A. Manuel Ferreira has chosen a curious title, NO REINO DE CAL-IBAN. Caliban is a Shakespearean character from THE TEMPEST; but it is necessary to understand who Caliban is. Caliban is an individual who lives in his own land and is captured by Europeans. Consequently, Caliban might apply to Brazil where there were Indians. Cape Verde, on the other hand, was unin-habited when the Europeans first came there. There were doves; Cape Verde was a land of peace! One cannot refer to Cape Verde as the Kingdom of Caliban. However, I am not de-nigrating the very important work of Manuel Ferreira.

Q. Manuel Ferreira chose his title as a metaphor for colonialism and the will of the colonized to cry out against his oppressor.

A. In Cape Verde there was no colonization. There was colonialism in Angola, in Sao Tome-Principe, in Mozambique, in Brazil, but not in Cape Verde. Colonialism is provoked by exploitation. There was nothing to exploit in Cape Verde. There were slaves who came to Cape Verde, but the slaves soon ceased being slaves and worked for themselves. The Portuguese took little interest in them.

Q. One of the principal themes in Cape Verdean literature is the dilemma of staying and struggling to make a living from an unyielding land or emigrating. This theme of exile exists in many African literatures, but the case of Cape Verde is special. You live in Portugal. In CHUVA BRAVA the hero, Mane Quim, chooses to stay in Cape Verde. Do you see any irony in this?

A. This is a universal problem. There are many Americans who live in France, who live in England. America is beautiful. The landscape in America is beautiful. Flying from Boston to New York I marvelled at the beauty of the coast. Rhode Island is so beautiful. When I ask Americans why they live elsewhere, they often say they want to have contact with different peoples. But foreigners come to America, I say. In my case as a civil servant the government sent me to the Acores, sent me to Portugal. It is the same with the English. They live throughout the world. Many civil servants settled in new lands. They may miss England and may return on holiday. But they find themselves comfortably settled outside of England. Cape Verde has 300,000 inhabitants. There are few professions there and agriculture is nearly impossible because of the lack of rainfall. The immigrants to the U.S. and Holland have regularly sent money back to their families in Cape Verde. But this has been cut back. I think the situation is transitory. We lived for forty years under a Portuguese dictatorship, although it was not a dictatorship created especially for Cape Verde. We suffered as a result of this dictatorship. Now the dictatorship in Cape Verde has been especially created for Cape Verdeans. I hope that this will change.

Q. Edicoes '70 in Lisbon has initiated a series of Cape Verdean works. CHUVA BRAVA and your collection of stories O GALO CANTOU NA BAIA (The Cock Crowed in the Bay) are the first two published works in this series. You wrote both of them many years ago. Yet you haven't produced a great deal since 1960.

A. I have been working on a revised edition of O GALO and that is the one Edicoes '70 has published. I have been working on stories and I continue to write poems and I like to paint. I find writing very hard work. Some days I don't write anything. Other days I'll work for five hours. Whoever said "Genius is 10% inspiration and 90% perspiration" was right. Gonsalves is now eighty.[7] He thinks he's twenty, that he has all the time in the world. He should write. He is such a fantastic story teller. But it's all in his head. I remember he once gave a series of two hour lectures on Balzac, without notes, and they were incredible. He could have continued giving lectures on Balzac, without notes for ten years without boring anyone. His knowledge of Eca de Queiros[8] is phenomenal. That man is a great scholar, but it's all in his head.

Q. You have written an essay on the artistic process of the novelist. This is something few African writers have done.

A. Yes. The novelist has a particular relationship with his characters. Some of his characters, I call these strong characters, have a life of their own. When I begin writing I do not know what a character will do. For instance in CHUVA BRAVA I have been accused by several readers of not marrying off Mane Quim and Escolastica, but I tell them that the problem is not mine. It is up to Mane Quim and Escolastica to get married if they wish. I have nothing to do with it. The actions of minor characters, on the other hand, are determined by events.

Q. There have been serious attempts in Cape Verde to create a "Crioulo" literature. Eugenio Tavares is perhaps the most celebrated Crioulo writer. Do you think a modern Crioulo literature can be created?

A. Crioulo does not have a written tradition. It doesn't have a grammar. We should be speaking not of a single Crioulo but of various Crioulos. Each island has its Crioulo language.

Q. Are there oral stories in Crioulo?

A. Yes, there are many: fables, stories. Just as Cape Verde was a new society, it created its own language. It simplified Portuguese for its own purposes. If a Portuguese goes to Cape Verde and hears Crioulo, he thinks it is an African language. But Dr. Baltasar Lopes has shown that, in fact, 97% of the vocabulary of Crioulo comes from Romance languages.

Q. Can Crioulo as a language express the soul of Cape Verde?

A. It certainly can. Conditions exist for that. To instutute Crioulo as a national language - I'm against that. It would limit the horizons of the Cape Verdean writer. But Crioulo has certain advantages over Portuguese. It is a more musical

language, a more lyrical language. Portuguese is a rather
harsh language.

YUSUF IDRIS

Along with Naguib Mahfouz, Yusuf Idris is in the forefront of modern Egyptian writing. While I was in Cairo, a full year after I had completed the other eleven interviews in this collection, I thought it would be a good idea to do an interview with Dr. Idris. I wanted very much to speak with an Egyptian writer, for I have the impression that Egyptian writing is not well known throughout the African continent. Moreover, at international conferences devoted to African literature, I do not recall many papers on Egyptian literature.

I had read THE CHEAPEST NIGHTS, a collection of stories written by Yusuf Idris when he was much younger, and I was impressed by his humor and his sketches of city life and country life. Today, Yusuf Idris is a columnist for the newspaper AL AHRAM.

This short interview, in English, took place in his office at AL AHRAM on Al Galaa Street in Cairo on the very hot afternoon of 31 May 1984.

YUSUF IDRIS

Q. I have interviewed a series of writers from West Africa,
East Africa and Central Africa, but you are the first
Egyptian writer I have spoken to. I am wondering if you
see Egyptian writing primarily in its Arabic context or do
you see Egyptian literature as part of an overall African
literature?

A. Egyptian literature cannot be seen independently from Arabic
literature in general. The main issues in Arabic literature
- what we call the great revolution in Arabic literature -
began after the Second World War. There are two principal
directions, both of which have the same purpose: bringing
Arabic literature away from an imitation of Western literature and expressing the spirit of the age in ultra modern
forms. This search for originality and the search for
modernism have combined to form one of the most powerful
literary expressions in the whole world. Unluckily the language barrier is great and it is a pity that the world cannot appreciate this great movement. In fact, the literary
movement is the source of the political movement. The Is-
raelis understand this. They are doing very well. They
study Arabic literature best. As a result they understand
the collective Arabic mentality, in particular the Egyptian
mentality. Especially one professor, an Iraqi Jew - I can't
remember his name - he is a professor of Arabic in the University at Jerusalem.

Q. You seem to suggest that Arabic critics are not doing their
job. Are they any good?

A. I wish I could say "yes," but they still follow traditional
Western ideas. We have yet to discover our original school
of literary criticism. We still try to apply Western rules
in literature. We still follow critics such as Belinsky.
In 1963 I advocated the development of an Egyptian theater.
The critics said, "No, it's not possible. There is only
European theater. Certainly you can fit the Egyptian experience into a European form. You can adapt this to Cairo."
But they were wrong. Yes, there is theater - in the customs
and lives of our people. The big five critics here in Egypt
took ten years to realize what I was saying. I was surprised
to hear Dr. Ali-al-Rayi, after visiting India and seeing so
many Indian plays, say, "It seems to me you are right. There
is a local theatrical community in the whole world."

Q. You alluded earlier to ultra-modernism. Isn't this going on
all over the world? Maybe Kafka started it, but you see it
everywhere. I'm thinking of Marquez, for instance.

A. Yes, everything is changing from direct statement to a per-
cussion-like effect of life on the reader. The symbolic,
the fantastic, the shocking way of telling things is the
modern way. We need Kafkalike stuff in our countries to
overcome great censorship. But it's not really Kafkalike.
Kafka is a fragment on the world stage. Hemingway, Chekhov
are fragments as well. Our main impression is from our folk-
lore, our innate literature.

Q. You are talking of oral literature.

A. Yes. We have had written literature dating from 1800. It
was very sluggish in movement. It didn't express the dreams
and fantasies of people. Oral literature was doing that.
Relating this to Arabic originality, you have to be inspired
by literature; you have to smell the originality.

Q. What caused this sluggishness of written literature? Was it
the tyranny of the Koran?

A. No. The Koran is powerful literature. It contains all the
musicality of the Arabic language. It's even ultra-modern
in some of its versions. The Koran is the most powerful
book of prose in Arabic literature. The sluggishness has resulted from Arabic literature being traditionally directed
to the ruling class - emirs, pashas, caliphs, princes. It
has been a formal literature, while popular literature is directed towards revolution of the human soul.

Q. You stated that the literary revolution in Arabic countries
anticipated political revolution. How is that so?

A. What is politics? The result of the trial of man - to go
from here to the future. What are the elements of this future? That is the field of literature. Literature stimu-
lates you to revolt from your present situation. It opens
windows to the future. And that's what politics does.

Q. What you're saying is very African. You're expressing an
idea shared by many African writers. Are you familiar with
African writers? For instance, do you know Dennis Brutus of
South Africa.

A. No. I'm not familiar with African literature. I do know a
Nigerian poet, a very aggressive poet. I can't remember his
name.

Q. "Aggressive" suggests J.P. Clark.

A. Yes, that's it. I met him in Moscow. Clark is very conceit-
ed. I also know of the playwright Soyinka. We were supposed
to meet at the University of Ibadan - for a conference on Af-

rican theater. That was three years ago. But the money never came through and I did not go. I was in Sweden last week. And they said he was there. Chasing the prize.

Q. Are you familiar with the English translation of your book of stories, THE CHEAPEST NIGHTS?

A. Yes. My short stories are written in what I call prose rhyming. This is different from poetic rhyme. The musicality of the language is not mere music; it has meaning. There is a need for the translator to write my stories as I would if I were writing in English. When Fitzgerald translated THE RUBAIYAT OF OMAR KHAYYAM, he wrote good poetry.

Q. He is a poet in his own right.

A. The translator must be. In the future translators of prose will be able to carry the musicality of the original language.

Q. We may have to wait a long time for that! I know at present you are interested more in drama than in short stories. How many plays have you written?

A. Ten. In fact, I have a meeting in a few minutes. We are trying to form a society of theater writers here. I'm sorry I do not have any more time to speak with you.

FOOTNOTES

1. Abafemi Awolowo - Head of United Party of Nigeria

2. Nnamdi Azikiwe - Head of Nigerian People's Party

3. Aminu Kano - Head of People's Redemption Party. He died shortly before the national elections in 1983.

4. A Nigerian staple food made from grains of cassava (gari) and hot water, eaten with sauce.

5. Chukwuemeka Odumegwu Ojukwu, former head of Biafra who went into exile in the Ivory Coast in January, 1970, and returned to Nigeria in July, 1982.

6. Sagres is a town on the Algarve coast in Southern Portugal, not far from Lagos.

7. The prose writer Antonio Aurelio Goncalves

8. Portuguese realistic novelist (1845-1900)

ISBN Prefix 0-89680-

Africa Series

16. Weisfelder, Richard F. THE BASOTHO MONARCHY: A Spent Force
     or a Dynamic Political Factor? 1972. 106 pp.
     049-0   (82-91676) $ 7.00*

19. Huntsberger, Paul E., compiler. HIGHLAND MOSAIC: A
     Critical Anthology of Ethiopian Literature in English.
     1973. 122 pp.
     052-0   (82-91700) $ 7.00*

21. Silberfein, Marilyn. CONSTRAINTS ON THE EXPANSION OF
     COMMERICAL AGRICULTURE: Iringa District, Tanzania.
     1974. 51 pp.
     054-7   (82-91726) $ 4.50*

22. Pieterse, Cosmo. ECHO AND CHORUSES: "Ballad of the Cells"
     and Selected Shorter Poems. 1974. 66 pp.
     055-5   (82-91734) $ 5.00*

23. Thom, Derrick J. THE NIGER-NIGERIA BOUNDARY: A
     Study of Ethnic Frontiers and a Colonial Boundary.
     1975. 50 pp.
     056-3   (82-91742) $ 4.75*

24. Baum, Edward compiler. A COMPREHENSIVE PERIODICAL BIBLIO-
     GRAPHY OF NIGERIA, 1960-1970. 1975. 250 pp.
     057-1   (82-91759) $13.00*

25. Kirchherr, Eugene C. ABYSSINIA TO ZIMBABWE: A Guide to the
     Political Units of Africa in the Period 1947-1978. 1979,
     3rd Ed. 80 pp.
     100-4   (82-91908) $ 8.00*

27. Fadiman, Jeffrey A. MOUNTAIN WARRIORS: The Pre-Colonial
     Meru of Mt. Kenya. 1976. 82 pp.
     060-1   (82-91783) $ 4.75*

32. Wright, Donald R. THE EARLY HISTORY OF THE NIUMI: Settle-
     ment and Foundation of a Mandinka State on the Gambia River.
     1977. 122 pp.
     064-4   (82-91833) $ 8.00*

36. Fadiman, Jeffrey A. THE MOMENT OF CONQUEST: Meru, Kenya,
     1907. 1979. 70 pp.
     081-4   (82-91874) $ 5.50*

37. Wright, Donald R. ORAL TRADITIONS FROM THE GAMBIA: Volume
     I, Mandinka Griots. 1979. 176 pp.
     083-0   (82-91882) $12.00*

38. Wright, Doanld R. ORAL TRADITIONS FROM THE GAMBIA: Volume
     II, Family Elders. 1980. 200 pp.
     064-9   (82-91890) $15.00*

39. Reining, Priscilla. CHALLENGING DESERTIFICATION IN WEST
     AFRICA: Insights from Landsat into Carrying Capacity,
     Cultivation and Settlement Site Identification in Upper
     Volta and Niger. 1979. 180 pp., illus.
     102-0   (82-91916) $12.00*

41. Lindfors, Bernth. MAZUNGUMZO: Interviews with East African
     Writers, Publishers, Editors, and Scholars. 1981. 179 pp.
     108-X   (82-91932) $13.00*

42. Spear, Thomas J. TRADITIONS OF ORIGIN AND THEIR INTERPRET-
     ATION: The Mijikenda of Kenya. 1982. xii, 163 pp.
     109-8   (82-91940) $13.50*

43. Harik, Elsa M. and Donald G. Schilling. THE POLITICS OF
     EDUCATION IN COLONIAL ALGERIA AND KENYA. 1984. 102 pp.
     117-9   (82-91957) $11.50*

44. Smith, Daniel R. THE INFLUENCE OF THE FABIAN COLONIAL
     BUREAU ON THE INDEPENDENCE MOVEMENT IN TANGANYIKA. 1985.
     x, 96 pp.
     125-X   (82-91965) $ 9.00*

45. Keto, C. Tsehloane. AMERICAN-SOUTH AFRICAN RELATIONS 1784-
     1980: Review and Select Bibliography. 1985. c. 174 pp.
     128-4   (82-91973) $11.00*

46. Burness, Don, and Mary-Lou Burness, ed. WANASEMA:
     Conversations with African Writers. 1985. c. 108 pp.
     129-2   (82-91981) $ 9.00*

47. Switzer, Les. MEDIA AND DEPENDENCY IN SOUTH AFRICA: A Case
     Study of the Press and the Ciskei "Homeland". 1985.
     c. 97 pp.
     130-6   (82-91999) $ 9.00*

Latin America Series

1.   Frei M., Eduardo. THE MANDATE OF HISTORY AND CHILE'S FUTURE.
     Tr. by Miguel d'Escoto. Intro. by Thomas Walker. 1977.
     79 pp.
     066-0   (82-92526) $ 8.00*

2.   Irish, Donald P., ed. MULTINATIONAL CORPORATIONS IN LATIN
     AMERICA: Private Rights--Public Responsibilities. 1978.
     135 pp.
     067-9   (82-92534) $ 9.00*

4. Martz, Mary Jeanne Reid. THE CENTRAL AMERICAN SOCCER WAR: Historical Patterns and Internal Dynamics of OAS Settlement Procedures. 1979. 118 pp.
   077-6   (82-92559) $ 8.00*

5. Wiarda, Howard J. CRITICAL ELECTIONS AND CRITICAL COUPS: State, Society, and the Military in the Processes of Latin American Development. 1979. 83 pp.
   082-2   (82-92567) $ 7.00*

6. Dietz, Henry A. and Richard Moore. POLITICAL PARTICIPATION IN A NON-ELECTORAL SETTING: The Urban Poor in Lima, Peru. 1979. viii, 102 pp.
   085-7   (82-92575) $ 9.00*

7. Hopgood, James F. SETTLERS OF BAJAVISTA: Social and Economic Adaptation in a Mexican Squatter Settlement. 1979. xii, 145 pp.
   101-2   (82-92583) $11.00*

8. Clayton, Lawrence A. CAULKERS AND CARPENTERS IN A NEW WORLD: The Shipyards of Colonial Guayaquil. 1980. 189 pp., illus.
   103-9   (82-92591) $15.00*

9. Tata, Robert J. STRUCTURAL CHANGES IN PUERTO RICO'S ECONOMY: 1947-1976. 1981. xiv, 104 pp.
   107-1   (82-92609) $11.75*

10. McCreery, David. DEVELOPMENT AND THE STATE IN REFORMA GUATEMALA, 1871-1885. 1983. viii, 120 pp.
    113-6   (82-92617) $ 8.50*

Southeast Asia Series

31. Nash, Manning. PEASANT CITIZENS: Politics, Religion, and Modernization in Kelantan, Malaysia. 1974. 181 pp.
    018-0   (82-90322) $12.00*

44. Collier, William L., et al. INCOME, EMPLOYMENT AND FOOD SYSTEMS IN JAVANESE COASTAL VILLAGES. 1977. 160 pp.
    031-8   (82-90454) $10.00*

47. Wessing, Robert. COSMOLOGY AND SOCIAL BEHAVIOR IN A WEST JAVANESE SETTLEMENT. 1978. 200 pp.
    072-5   (82-90488) $12.00*

48. Willer, Thomas F., ed. SOUTHEAST ASIAN REFERENCES IN THE BRITISH PARLIAMENTARY PAPERS, 1801-1972/73: An Index. 1977. 110 pp.
    033-4   (82-90496) $ 8.50*

50. Echauz, Robustiano. SKETCHES OF THE ISLAND OF NEGROS.
    1978. 174 pp.
    070-9   (82-90512) $10.00*

51. Krannich, Ronald L. MAYORS AND MANAGERS IN THAILAND: The
    Struggle for Political Life in Administrative Settings.
    1978. 139 pp.
    073-3   (82-90520) $ 9.00*

52. Davis, Glora, ed. WHAT IS MODERN INDONESIAN CULTURE? 1978.
    300 pp.
    075-X   (82-90538) $18.00*

54. Ayal, Eliezar B., ed. THE STUDY OF THAILAND: Analyses of
    Knowledge, Approaches, and Prospects in Anthropology, Art
    History, Economics, History and Political Science. 1979.
    257 pp.
    079-2   (82-90553) $13.50*

56. Duiker, William J. VIETNAM SINCE THE FALL OF SAIGON.
    Second Edition, Revised and Enlarged. 1985. c. 300 pp.
    133-0   (82-90744) $12.00*

57. Siregar, Susan Rodgers. ADAT, ISLAM, AND CHRISTIANITY IN A
    BATAK HOMELAND. 1981. 108 pp.
    110-1   (82-90587) $10.00*

58. Van Esterik, Penny. COGNITION AND DESIGN PRODUCTION IN BAN
    CHIANG POTTERY. 1981. 90 pp.
    076-4   (82-90595) $12.00*

59. Foster, Brian L. COMMERCE AND ETHNIC DIFFERENCES: The Case
    of the Mons in Thailand. 1982. x, 93 pp.
    112-8   (82-90603) $10.00*

60. Frederick, William H. and John H. McGlynn. REFLECTIONS ON
    REBELLION: Stories from the Indonesian Upheavals of 1948
    and 1965. 1983. vi, 168 pp.
    111-X   (82-90611) $ 9.00*

61. Cady, John F. CONTACTS WITH BURMA. 1935-1949: A Personal
    Account. 1983. x, 117 pp.
    114-4   (82-90629) $ 9.00*

62. Kipp, Rita Smith and Richard D. Kipp, eds. BEYOND SAMOSIR:
    Recent Studies of the Batak Peoples of Sumatra. 1983.
    viii, 155 pp.
    115-2   (82-90637) $ 9.00*

63. Carstens, Sharon, ed. CULTURAL IDENTITY IN NORTHERN
    PENINSULAR MALAYSIA. 1985. c. 109 pp.
    116-0   (82-90645) $ 9.00*

64. Dardjowidjojo, Soenjono. VOCABULARY BUILDING IN INDONESIAN:
    An Advanced Reader. 1984. xviii, 256 pp.
    118-7   (82-90652) $18.00*

65. Errington, J. Joseph. LANGUAGE AND SOCIAL CHANGE IN JAVA:
    Linguistic Reflexes of Modernization in a Traditional Royal
    Polity. 1985. xiv, 198 pp.
    120-9   (82-90660) $12.00*

66. Binh, Tran Tu. THE RED EARTH: A Vietnamese Memoir of Life
    on a Colonial Rubber Plantation. Tr. by John Spragens.
    Ed. by David Marr. 1985. xii, 98 pp.
    119-5   (82-90678) $ 9.00*

67. Pane, Armijn. SHACKLES. Tr. by John McGlynn. Intro. by
    William H. Frederick. 1985. xvi, 108 pp.
    122-5   (82-90686) $ 9.00*

68. Syukri, Ibrahim. HISTORY OF THE MALAY KINGDOM OF PATANI.
    Tr. by Conner Bailey and John N. Miksic. 1985. xx, 98 pp.
    123-3   (82-90694) $10.50*

69. Keeler, Ward. JAVANESE: A Cultural Approach. 1984.
    xxxvi, 523 pp.
    121-7   (82-90702) $18.00*

70. Wilson, Constance M. and Lucien M. Hanks. BURMA-THAILAND
    FRONTIER OVER SIXTEEN DECADES: Three Descriptive Documents.
    1985. x, 128 pp.
    124-1   (82-90710)   forthcoming $10.50*

71. Thomas, Lynn L. and Franz von Benda-Beckmann, eds. CHANGE
    AND CONTINUITY IN MINANGKABAU: Local, Regional, and
    Historical Perspectives on West Sumatra. 1985. c. 360 pp.
    127-6   (82-90728)   forthcoming $14.00*

72. Reid, Anthony and Oki Akira, eds. THE JAPANESE EXPERIENCE
    IN INDONESIA: Selected Memoirs of 1942-1945. 1985.
    c. 450 pp., 20 illus.
    132-2   (82-90736)   forthcoming $18.00*

                        ORDERING INFORMATION

     Orders for titles in the Monographs in International Studies
series should be placed through the Ohio University Press/Scott
Quadrangle/Athens, Ohio, 45701-2979. Individuals must remit
prepayment via check, VISA, MasterCard, CHOICE, or American
Express. Individuals ordering from outside of the U.S. please
remit in U.S. funds by either International Money Order or check
drawn on a U.S. bank. Residents of Ohio and Missouri please add
sales tax. Postage and handling is $2.00 for the first book and
$.50 for each additional book. Prices and availability are
subject to change without notice.